DARKNESS IS ONLY LIGHT NOT SWITCHED ON

(Walking with Angels)

BY JEANNE AMES

© Copyright 2005 Jeanne Ames.

All rights reserved. No part of this publication may be reproduced, stored in a retrieval system, or transmitted, in any form or by any means, electronic, mechanical, photocopying, recording, or otherwise, without the written prior permission of the author.

Note for Librarians: a cataloguing record for this book that includes Dewey Decimal Classification and US Library of Congress numbers is available from the Library and Archives of Canada. The complete cataloguing record can be obtained from their online database at:
www.collectionscanada.ca/amicus/index-e.html
ISBN 1-4120-5508-3

Printed in Victoria, BC, Canada

 *Printed on paper with minimum 30% recycled fibre. Trafford's print shop runs on "green energy" from solar, wind and other environmentally-friendly power sources.*

TRAFFORD
Offices in Canada, USA, Ireland and UK

This book was published *on-demand* in cooperation with Trafford Publishing. On-demand publishing is a unique process and service of making a book available for retail sale to the public taking advantage of on-demand manufacturing and Internet marketing. On-demand publishing includes promotions, retail sales, manufacturing, order fulfilment, accounting and collecting royalties on behalf of the author.

Book sales for North America and international:
Trafford Publishing, 6E–2333 Government St.,
Victoria, BC v8t 4p4 CANADA
phone 250 383 6864 (toll-free 1 888 232 4444)
fax 250 383 6804; email to orders@trafford.com

Book sales in Europe:
Trafford Publishing (uk) Ltd., Enterprise House, Wistaston Road Business Centre,
Wistaston Road, Crewe, Cheshire cw2 7rp UNITED KINGDOM
phone 01270 251 396 (local rate 0845 230 9601)
facsimile 01270 254 983; orders.uk@trafford.com
Order online at:
trafford.com/05-0406

10 9 8 7 6 5 4 3 2

Contents

Introduction / Prologue	5
1 Beginning the Journey	9
2 Co-incidences	15
3 My Introduction to Healing	23
4 Expanding wisdom into understanding	32
5 Negatives	40
6 Birth Frequency Healing and Flower Essences	50
7 Birth Frequency Healing and the Three Musketeers	63
8 Proof of the Pudding and Australia	76
9 Communicating with Masters and Angels	87
10 Angels and Esoteric Acupuncture	100
11 The manifestation of my affirmations after the Clown Exercise	110
12 A return trip to Australia and flying with a new group of Angels!	119
13 Walking back to Life	131
Acknowledgements	141

Introduction / Prologue

I've held various positions in my life, including that of personal secretary, stable girl, fish fryer, and shop assistant, to name but a few. Although these occupations helped shape me into the person I am today, my life changed most drastically when I became a healer.

It all began in 1993 when I visited a tarot reader and spiritual medium and was told unequivocally that I was a healer. This was subsequently repeated to me by another medium at the spiritual church, and again by a woman sitting behind me at a course I was attending. All these encounters took place in the space of six months.

For the next ten years, I stumbled blindly, trying to find my way. Things gradually became clear after I experienced several carefully orchestrated encounters with several entities, which helped change my perceptions of myself and of life on earth. When I relayed the stories of my visits from these energies and angels to people, they would invariably ask me if I had been afraid. Upon reflection, I would reply that the experiences actually had the opposite effect; I had suddenly felt incredibly calm.

This amazing journey entailed periods of great sadness, despair, loneliness, and deep introspection, interspersed with moments of exhilaration and excitement that words could never describe. Throughout the journey, I witnessed more than one miracle with the help of the healing system I have created, not the least of which was my own miracle.

In January 2002, in the space of one hour, I died twice and was revived. I spent the next five days in a coma on life support and three weeks in the cardiac care unit of the Norfolk and Norwich Hospital. I was eventually diagnosed with acute inflated viral cardiomyopathy. Before I was discharged from hospital, I asked a nurse if my condition could be reversed. Her facial expression immediately changed. After flashing me the look of a veteran who had dealt with many such cases, she said firmly but gently "No."

It is now February 2003. I had an angiogram last October 2002 that revealed my enlarged heart had returned to normal size. All that could be found to explain my condition in January 2002 was a furring of the arteries, which didn't explain the events of my illness, the symptoms, or the diagnosis. The consultant who performed my angiogram at the Norfolk and Norwich Hospital was left scratching his head in confusion. He sent me to Papworth to see a specialist, who described my recovery as 'miraculous.' As I had no angina and no symptoms, the specialist recommended I control my cholesterol level with medication. That was it. There was no need for a bypass or any other surgery.

What I have been unable to convey to any of these wonderful doctors is that I was able to help myself by using my system of healing and my knowledge of holistic healing. I enlisted the help of my students to use on me what I had taught them, and was told by my Angel friends to visit a man I had met some four years earlier and ask for help. The healing modalities I use are simple and easy to use. So simple and easy, in fact, that anyone can be taught to use them safely.

The hardest part has been locating the emotional root of my disease. As a healer, I had learned that glaucoma was equated with tunnel vision regarding certain aspects of a person's life. If cystitis occurs, it means the person is 'pissed off' about something. Sinusitis means something is 'getting up a person's nose.' I needed to discover the emotional root of my disease.

All human beings are born with a blueprint commonly known as DNA. This blueprint not only creates the human body using a chemical messaging system, but also forms the basis of the body's cellular renewal and repair system from birth to death. Most humans fail to look at the miracle of our creation. They don't understand how our skin heals when it's cut, or how our body is able to create cells programmed to recognize the DNA or RNA of an invading virus and then locate and destroy that virus (our immune system.)

The human body is a complex multifunctional organism. The fact that every cell has a memory has been demonstrated time and again by transplant patients reporting incidents post transplant, such as having a sudden liking for football or Chinese food, despite hating it pre-transplant. This cellular memory is constantly running programmes, much like a computer, and unless counselling is given in a knowledgeable and specific way, the old programming will either recreate the old disease or a new one will eventually manifest.

In my experience, there is no way of bypassing the system our bodies have of signalling to us that we need emotional healing. It is this part of the healing process that is so difficult to bring about. Moreover, the process is different for each individual. So, for all the people who heal by offering up a prayer, yes, this often works and God knows I have offered up a few myself in my time; however, when it comes to completely healing, a little knowledge or a hit and miss attitude just isn't good enough. I thank my lucky stars it isn't. I would hate to experience life within the confines of a damaged heart, short of breath and unable to do the things I love. When I came out of hospital, I told everybody that if I couldn't do anything like walk my dogs or ride a horse, I wasn't staying.

With my healing knowledge and my friends' help in applying my knowledge and theirs, I was able to return to a normal life. Of course, I'll be forever grateful to my Angels, who have never failed to respond to my calls for help.

CHAPTER 1

Beginning the Journey

I was born in February 1950. At the time of my birth, my father was a lorry driver. We lived in a small rented house not far from my grandmother Mary. My father's family was a closely knit group ruled by Mary's loving but stern hand. My father left school at the age of fourteen and began working as a driver's mate before becoming a lorry driver. One day he came home and proudly announced he had been chosen as the new foreman. I idolized my father; he was the one person with whom I always felt safe. He constantly told me I was the apple of his eye and that he loved me so much I could have his last breath.

My mum was a very shy and quiet individual who loved and believed in my father. He was her boss, provider, and protector -- roles he relished. My mother's parents died within a week of each other when she was fourteen. She had five brothers and sisters. We were not as close to this side of the family, although everyone met at Christmas and at regular intervals during the year. As a result of the sudden unexpected loss of her parents at such an early age, Mum took to motherhood with relish. She loved me and cherished me with a fervour, which made me feel so safe and secure I never wanted to leave the safety of my home, even with aunts or uncles. When my mother dropped me off at my new school at the age of five, I took one quick look around, decided I didn't like the teacher or anyone else, and headed back out the door and down the street. It didn't even enter my head to be afraid of the big wide world without a parent in tow; all I could think of was getting back to the safety of my home with Mum.

When I arrived home, I found Mum sitting at the kitchen table with her head in her hands, sobbing. When I asked her what was wrong, she said leaving me at school had made her very sad. She said she didn't like us to be apart, and the thought of my growing up scared her. From then on, it was a battle to get me to go to school every day. I became such an expert at feigning illness that I often fooled Mum.

After Dad's job change, we bought a house, which meant a change of school for me. Once more, I was forced into an environment full of total strangers. All day Sunday I would dread having to return to school the next morning. After awhile, though, I made new friends, and my parents allowed me to have a dog, something I had wanted since the age of two. Life began to settle and although money was short, things began to improve significantly.

Just when I was beginning to feel settled, Dad came home with the news that he had done such a good job of running the new Norwich Depot, he had been offered a promotion to Manager. The only problem was that the job would entail a move 200 miles away to Loughborough. Until he had sold the house in Norwich and could find a house to buy, he would have to travel to Loughborough every Monday morning and return on Friday. I viewed the move with the same dread as Mum. She was being ripped from the bosom of her family, and I was being forced into another new school with strangers, away from the familiarity, strength, and support of Grandmother Mary and my aunts and uncles.

It never ceased to amaze me that although my father had left school at fourteen with only a very rudimentary education, he was still able to rise through the ranks at his company with apparent ease and excel in every job he had. The one basic rule he would always stress to me was 'Keep it simple." This rule, combined with some good old-fashioned common sense, enabled my father to rise to the post of Operations Manager. I, too, have applied this rule to everything I have done in my life, and it has always served me well.

After our move to Loughborough, I was faced with an introduction to yet another new school and a new bunch of strangers. The system of teaching in Loughborough was totally different from that in Norwich, and I struggled.

After a few months, I began to make new friends and settle in. When I returned to school after our summer break, I expected to be moved up to year four with all my friends. Instead, I was told to see the headmaster, who informed me that I would have to repeat year three again. Once again, I found myself in a classroom full of strangers, but with the added humiliation of believing that I wasn't clever enough to go into year four and having to be separated from my friends. I felt like I was being punished and that I'd let my parents down. As always, my father had words of comfort, but I knew his views were tainted by his love for me. I believed he was telling me what I wanted to hear so I wouldn't be hurt by the truth.

I had developed this belief system early in my formative years, when I was about three or four. One incident in particular sticks in my memory. Even as a toddler, I demonstrated a great love for animals. We had a family cat that disappeared one day. When I asked Mum where my beloved cat was, she told me it had disappeared. That night I dreamed my father had killed the cat by laying a blanket over it. It was only when I relayed this dream to Mum that she finally admitted that Dad had taken the cat to the vet and it had been put down because it had cancer. She thought that if she told me the cat was missing, it wouldn't bother me. She had lied to save me the pain of knowing my cat was dead.

From that day forward, I began to feel somewhat isolated, even from my parents. That dream had shown me the truth of the situation, contrary to my parent's desires. I'll never forget the anguish on Mum's face when she realized she would have to tell me the truth and witness my hurt. I blamed myself for her anguish.

When TV first became a household appliance and the game shows came on, I would often be able to answer the questions. I had no idea how I knew these answers; they would just pop into my head. On one occasion, the answer to a question was Venezuela. I voiced the answer to the question out loud and clear. What on earth are you talking about, Jean? I thought to myself. However as usual, my answer was correct. Mum was sitting right beside me at the time and didn't bat an eyelash. She had become used to such goings on, and turned a blind eye to her strange child's ability to utter words she had never heard before and answer questions far beyond her years and knowledge.

I always had an innate ability to read what people were thinking. I was painfully shy, spoiled, and protected, and I knew people thought I was a spoiled brat. I didn't like my ability to tune into people and their thoughts and feelings. I didn't like the dreams that made my mother uncomfortable. She was always uncomfortable when I inexplicably answered questions on the TV and sometimes her unspoken questions. She never said anything to me, but often remarked to people that I was a strange child. So, in an effort to become normal, I tried to switch off all these strange abilities I seemed to possess. I never told anyone about my premonitions and stopped vocalizing the answers to questions. By the age of seven, my abilities seemed to have disappeared, or at least I didn't notice them as much.

We moved from Loughborough to London. What a culture shock that was! My new school was full of aggressive teenagers. Ever mindful of his deprived childhood and lack of schooling, my dad bought me the entire school uniform, including the blazer. I remember having to wear huge round-toed, sensible shoes instead of the winkle pickers that were the fashion at the time. This led to my being the subject of much ridicule and laughter. In particular, I remember a very large girl by the name of Mary, who took to making fun of me. I pleaded with Mum and Dad to let me have a pair of winkle pickers so I could look like the rest of the children. Eventually, I also managed to leave the blazer at home without Mum noticing.

I excelled at my new school in London and was soon ranked in the top six in the highest grade. I dreaded having to leave school and face life as an adult. Every time the thought arose, I buried it as deep as I could and tried not to think about the future.

The day finally arrived when I finished my exams and left school. My first job was as a secretary in a large loans company. By now I had acquired ownership of my first horse. Her name was Sema, my surname spelled backwards. I bought Sema because I liked her spirit. I also enjoyed riding really difficult horses; so much so, in fact, that the people at the stables where I kept her would ask me to ride their difficult horses for them. I loved riding these animals. I would always know what they were going to do seconds before they did it. I think most riders would also attest to this ability without looking for any deeper understanding of it.

Sema was extremely thin but had a very fat belly. She was very aggressive towards other horses. After about two months, I began to suspect she was in foal. When I mentioned this to Roy, her previous owner (and the owner of the stables where I kept her), he laughed at me. Another month went by and Sema's condition still had not improved. No one would believe she was in foal. Frustrated, I called a vet and asked him to examine her. Before the examination, he announced that there was no way she was in foal; he could tell by just looking at her. I insisted on an examination anyway. As soon as he inserted his fist, he came in contact with the fetus. He gave Sema a 50/50 chance of survival, based on the poor state of her health.

What had I learned so far? What conditioned imprint had I placed in my cellular patterning that would influence my response in all future situations? You see, we have brain memory and cellular memory, both of which have to be cleared of imbalances in order to remove old patterns that create 'dis-ease' within us. If a disease manifests in our bodies, one of the secrets of reversing the process of that disease is to look at what we are not at ease with in our lives.

I learned:
(1) My early years were spent encircled, comforted, and protected from everything. My parents' constant efforts to protect me and ensure my safety made me distrustful of strangers and the world in general.
(2) I had a duty to take care of myself for the sake of my parents and run my life in a way that would never upset them. It was not just my life for which I was responsible; I was also responsible for my parents' happiness. If I made a mistake or was injured, I would cause them great sadness.
(3) I learned to switch off my inner guidance -- that sixth sense we all take for granted -- after the dream about the cat and Mum's comments inferring I wasn't normal. I learned to switch off my visionary capabilities that made people view me with suspicion and fear.
(4) I experienced the pain of loss and death, which served to install a deep-rooted fear of the pain of loss. Most importantly, I knew that in the future I would likely have to face the pain of losing my grandmother, mother, and father when age took its toll. I feared the future.
(5) I was gradually establishing a view that this earth was a painful and difficult place in which to live.
(6) I learned to KEEP IT SIMPLE
(7) I learned that basic common sense always provides an answer quickly, no matter how daft or simple this may seem.
What was the universe trying to teach me by introducing certain events into my life?

Moving and changing schools repeatedly put me in situations with strangers where I had to accept new things. I had a choice to accept the learning and be adaptable or be angry at the universe, my life, and myself. The universe was giving me situations from which I could learn and clear the cellular pattern my parents had helped create by teaching me that the only safe place was home and family. I chose my responses to each environment. In hindsight, this is easy to see; however, it was not so easy at the time. The universe was also putting in place the qualities I needed to create the system of healing that would eventually restore my health. I chose anger and hid behind a façade of aggression. That was what Dad taught me, and he was my hero and role model.

CHAPTER 2

Co-incidences

After three people had told me I was a healer, I began my journey into healing. At first I had no idea where to start. I had been so busy surviving the past forty years in this painful, dangerous place called earth that I didn't think to go to a library to search for books on healing. None of the people who had told me I was a healer offered any suggestions as to how I could learn; they seemed to think I already knew. At the time, I didn't have the good sense to ask for help for fear of being thought of as stupid. (Later, some Australian friends would show me that it was okay to ask for help and that there was no point in being timid.)

At this point in my life, I had met a young man named Roger, who was 18 years younger than me. He had his work cut out for him in creating any sort of relationship with me. I had been married twice and had two children – Iain and Marie – from my second marriage.

Iain's birth had been difficult, resulting in my first experience in hospital in a life-or-death situation. The birth was by emergency caesarean 32 weeks into the pregnancy. My husband at the time had chosen to go away for the weekend while I was hospitalized. When informed of the premature birth, he decided it wasn't important enough for him to return. Instead, he went out to celebrate his son's birth and was too drunk to return for twenty-four hours.

My mum visited me at the hospital that day. She was beside me on one side of the bed and a nurse was permanently positioned on the other side to monitor my blood pressure. Mum attempted to look unconcerned, furiously clicking her knitting needles as she knitted yet another jumper for the new baby. I placed my hand on her arm and told her not to worry, that I would be okay. I had no idea where this inspiration had come from, but I felt strangely calm. My only worry was that my baby hadn't moved inside me for thirty-six hours. That evening, the consultant in charge came off his weekend break, took one look at my records, and announced that my baby would be born that night by caesarean section. Luckily, I had not eaten all day. Something had told me I would need an anaesthetic, and I wanted no delays in getting the baby out of that dangerous place -- my womb. I vividly remember waking up and being shown a photograph of my son. As soon as I saw him, I knew his name would be Iain. I spent the next two days in intensive care with my life hanging in the balance until my blood pressure was finally under control.

My first visitor was my Dad, who cried openly and told me the story of how he had been told there was a 50/50 chance that either the baby or I would survive. During the two-hour operation, he and my mum had sat in their parked car staring at the eighth floor and waiting for the lights to go out, a sign that the operation was over. What have I put them through? I thought, vowing never to do it again. In fact, the first thing my Dad said to me was, "Don't do it again, please."

My husband's treatment of me only served to strengthen my belief that only family really cares about you, that blood is thicker than water, that you really cannot trust others like you can your family. Our relationship was a tempestuous one. He became a drug addict. I also caught him in many affairs, and he was often violent. I valiantly stood up for myself the way Dad had taught me, but it always made things worse and probably increased the number of beatings I received. I refused to succumb to control by violence or fear. We were now divorced, but I refused to acknowledge my fear I experienced every time I heard a car pull up in the driveway. As a result, I developed a very nasty eczema rash all the way up my arm.

On one occasion after a particularly bad beating, during which I had incurred two black eyes, I was able to go to court and get an injunction with a power of arrest attached to stop my ex-husband coming within ten miles of my house. The case actually set a precedent in legal history at the time, as I was no longer married to him and therefore not entitled to such an injunction. I would later take civil action on that injunction.

I had just accepted a job serving in a fish and chip shop. I started on the Friday night and was due in court on the civil case against my ex-husband the following Monday morning. My only problem with working in a shop was that he might suddenly walk in. I consoled myself with the fact that he did not like fish and chips and lived on the other side of town.

As luck would have it, my ex-husband was the first customer I served. His astonishment at finding me working in the shop was matched only by my own surprise at seeing him. He was waiting for me when I left. He had parked his car behind mine so I couldn't get in my car and drive away. The 'coincidence' had fueled his belief that we were destined for each other and that the bond between us was too strong to be broken. He chose to ignore the fact that he was living with another woman at the time. Ours had been a deep love and I had trusted him enough to allow myself to become pregnant. Although he had demonstrated time and again that he was unreliable, violent, untrustworthy, a control freak, I couldn't seem to find the strength to escape him.

The death of my father was to be the turning point in my relationship with my ex-husband. Within weeks of Dad's death, I had received another black eye. This time there was no one there to listen to or rescue me. The only way I could move forward was to eradicate the violence and control in my life. I found the resolve to reject him again and again. After a short while I met Roger.

Although younger than I, Roger was mature far beyond his years. With his help, I began to relax and feel safe. It was during my time with Roger that I first went to see the tarot reader and medium who told me to go out and start healing. One of Roger's friends ran a shop that sold tarot cards and crystals. I had always thought this friend a bit strange, and attributed her belief that a crystal around her neck had eradicated her eczema to the silliness of youth. After seeing the tarot reader and being suitably impressed by what she knew about me (even down to photographs I had on the wall), I became fascinated by the thought there might actually be spirits who came to visit, not the least of which were my mum and dad. Mum had died of a massive heart attack in 1979, six days before my daughter Marie was born. She had been looking after me at the time because I had been to court to get my husband removed from my house, as his behaviour was threatening my health and that of my baby. Mum had moved to Norwich from London to look after me.

I was now fuelled by a curiosity I could not quell. I visited the shop where Roger's friend worked and looked at some tarot cards. I had no intentions of buying anything, but I left the shop with a set of tarot cards, a silk scarf, and a book. From that point on, I became obsessed with the tarot deck and spent hours doing different spreads for myself. After a few weeks, I began doing readings for friends. Everything came to me quite easily; I seemed to have a natural affinity for it. More importantly, though, the tarot deck caused me to question myself and my life. It forced me to look at myself, and I didn't like what I saw.

Jeanne Ames

Some months later when I was looking through tarot cards at a shop in Norwich, I was drawn to a particular deck called the Power deck. Impulsively, I told the girl in the shop I wanted to buy the deck. She told me they were not ordinary or normal tarot cards. Attempting to display confidence, I told her I was aware of this. (Of course, I knew no such thing!) I took these new cards home and immediately drew one that said, "Look for the power in the stone." Okay, I'll give these crystals a go, I thought. While in Norwich, I found myself purchasing a small quartz point crystal that cost £1. Money was extremely tight at the time, and I chastised myself for being stupid enough to have spent much needed cash on such a silly thing.

I forgot all about the crystal until that evening when I removed it from the paper bag. As I rubbed the crystal between the thumb and forefinger of both hands, it suddenly lit up. I felt a pulsating energy flowing through my thumbs. A shimmering light emanated from the fingers touching the crystal, forming a filmy shadow of light in the shape of a figure of eight. When I looked closely, I could see outlines in the crystal. I had no idea what these outlines were. I didn't understand what was happening, but I decided there must be something to this crystal healing after all.

It was about this time that I made friends with a girl named Lucy. She was also interested in this esoteric stuff. On weekends we would go to psychic fairs and the like. One weekend she rang me looking for something to do. I told her my friend June had told me about a psychic fair in Yarmouth and that I would phone June for more details. June wasn't home when I called, so I phoned another friend, Jackie, who said the fairs were normally held at a hotel in Yarmouth. I spent the next few hours doing housework and forgot all about the psychic fair until that afternoon when I decided to call the hotel Jackie had given me to see if there was a fair on. I racked my brain, trying to remember the name. Finally it came to me -- the Star Hotel.

Lucy and I set off for Yarmouth and found the Star Hotel. By now my obsession with tarot and the supernatural had grown to include a fascination for crystals. Certain crystals created vibrations in my hands, which fuelled my fascination. As we walked around the fair, I was drawn to a large crystal ball in which I could see the shape of an eagle inside. When I tentatively enquired about the price of the crystal ball, I was told it was £60.00. I couldn't justify such a purchase, as it had been only a matter of weeks since I had bought the first £1 crystal. I eventually paid for the crystal by credit card, leaving the problem of how the bill would be paid for another day. On the way home we dropped in to see Jackie, who saw my acquisition and asked where I had bought it. I told her I had bought it at the Star Hotel, where she had told me to go. She looked somewhat surprised and said she had never told me to go to the Star Hotel. In fact, she had never known the Star Hotel to hold psychic fairs; they were usually held at the Imperial Hotel, where she had told me to go. How had I known to go to the Star Hotel?

It was around this time that my cousin's wife Betty heard about my new-found interest and invited me to a séance. She told me her friend from the spiritualist church would be there and that her guide would make sure we didn't get any nasty spirits. Reassured by this, I agreed to attend. Roger declined to go and dropped me off. As we all sat around the table, the glass began to move. When asked if there was a message for anyone, it spelled my name. I don't remember what the message was, but when I asked the name of the spirit that was present, the glass spelled the word 'William.' When asked who William was, it spelled 'grandfather.'

Although I didn't realize it at the time, I was pregnant with Roger's child. When I got home I phoned my aunt and questioned her about the names of my grandparents. None of them was named William. After I told Iain and Marie about my experience, they asked if we could try a séance, to which I reluctantly agreed. Immediately the glass spelled out the name William, and again it said 'grandfather.' It began to tell us things like the dog had eaten food off the desk. Sure enough, when we checked, the pork chops for the evening meal had disappeared and a guilty looking dog was sitting in the middle of the room.

One evening during a séance, the spirit spelled out the name of my ex-husband and informed us that he was coming. At this point, all my dogs began barking. The children and I looked at each other, gripped by fear. Iain locked all the doors, I told him to go upstairs and shout out the window to see if anyone was about. This he duly did and got no reply. The glass then spelled out 'You are angry.'

"Yes! You're frightening us," I said out loud.

The glass moved again, spelling out 'He is in the hayshed.' Again, Iain went upstairs and shouted out the window. Still no reply. The dogs continued to bark for a while.

About three days later, my ex-husband turned up in the daytime. Iain went outside to see him. He had come to get his ladders, which Iain had moved from the hayshed a few days earlier. When Iain asked him if he had he been there the night of our séance, his obvious shock at the question gave him away. Because he thought I wouldn't let him have the ladders, he had come under the cover of darkness and searched for them in the hayshed, from where Iain had removed them.

The séances continued for a while. I would often conduct a séance when I was on my own. It was on one such occasion that William told me he was Roger's father. Roger had never mentioned his father except to say that when Roger was eighteen, his father had died a long and painful death from cancer. As a result, Roger had a strong dislike for hospitals and didn't believe there was a God because his father had suffered so much. From that point on, his father had become a taboo subject.

I soon began speaking to William without the aid of a glass to spell out words. It was as if a voice in my head were speaking to me. At first I thought I had imagined it. I knew instinctively that I should tell Roger about the mystery spirit. He had never mentioned his father's name, so I asked him what it was. He told me it was William. When I replied that William was the spirit who had come through in the séance, Roger said, "Thank you." and that was it.

One day, during a séance, William told us to put everything away and never perform séances again. We were so frightened we never did. But I had discovered I no longer needed the glass; the communication was direct.

I was becoming more and more insecure in my relationship with Roger. He tried to talk to me and was always asking if I was happy. I always lied and said I was, when really I was afraid he would leave me. That age-old fear of mine that living things you love eventually leave kept rearing its ugly head. When arguments arose, I would test his loyalty by telling him to leave if he wanted. He began to think I didn't want him. I refused to expose my vulnerability the way I had done with my ex-husband. No one was ever going to do that to me again. This attitude eventually caused Roger to leave and never return.

I was on my own again. Within a week, my ex husband was knocking on my door. I waited for Roger to return. I even wrote him a couple of letters. My tarot cards had advised me to 'give the facts to get what you want.' I told Roger that I still loved and missed him. I was learning about myself and was beginning to change, thanks to a set of cards. Was it a coincidence that I had met Roger at a time in my life when I needed strength to keep my ex-husband away? Was it a coincidence that I had found out about William at the séance, or that I had begun to pick up messages from spirit and knew how to tune in and listen? Was all this coincidental or accidental?

Even my first visit to the spiritual medium and tarot reader had occurred in a mystical way. Two friends who knew nothing about each other had simultaneously booked me in for an appointment with the same tarot reader. What had I learned from this chapter of my life?

(1) All the intuition I had possessed since childhood -- knowing answers to questions or that certain events would take place – was a real part of me, and it was okay to acknowledge this. It didn't mean I was strange or abnormal. I began to accept it as a true gift and not a curse.

(2) I learned that men are control freaks who dominate by using threats, violence, and emotional blackmail.

(3) I learned not to be vulnerable, or at least not to show my vulnerability.

(4) I learned to be tough and strong. I was a single parent raising two small children on my own.

(5) I learned that life was full of strange coincidences.

What was the universe trying to teach me?

There are no coincidences. Every experience is an opportunity to learn on our journey. Each individual is free to take that learning, ingest it, and then create whatever pattern they choose to experience life. What seems like cruel fate can in fact be an opportunity to change the future, if we are a little introspective, honest, and true to ourselves. I had not yet come to terms with the fact that I was choosing these painful learning situations. That was too awful to contemplate and seemed stupid. I still believed that life is shit and then you die.

CHAPTER 3

My Introduction to Healing

Roger had left and not returned or contacted us. Apart from Iain and Marie, I was alone again. Marie was out with her boyfriend, Toby most of the time, so Iain and I started attending meetings run by the medium and tarot reader I had first seen. She would give messages to people and talk about different spiritual topics. At one of these meetings, she invited a man to talk about a particular system of healing known as Reiki. He described how healers normally felt drained after a healing, and how Reiki plugged you into universal energy that flowed freely through you. It required some sets of attunements, the first set of which you acquired during a two-day course, and the second set, over two half-days. After acquiring an attunement called 3a and a set of four attunements, you became a Reiki Master. The first-degree course was £180.00. I immediately thought it was just a money-making scheme. My friend June was with me at this meeting. When we left, she announced she was attending a meeting where someone was giving a talk about Reiki. I reluctantly agreed to accompany her.

We arrived at the talk and were introduced to a man named Jason, to whom I took an immediate dislike. I had no real reason to dislike this man, apart from his arrogance and rather chauvinistic attitude towards women. He spoke about the Reiki and told us we couldn't just 'get Reiki'; we had to take an attunement. Only a Reiki Master could give you such an attunement. The Reiki Master had to have gone through the levels of attunement on his way to becoming a Master before being able to attune others using symbols. We didn't need to learn anything; when we accepted the attunements, the energy would always flow freely, even if we were unconscious.

I left the talk unconvinced. My friend June, however, was enthusiastic and immediately signed up for the course. It took me another two weeks to make my decision. What clinched it for me was the fact that my cards had told me a golden opportunity would present itself and that I should seize that opportunity. As far as I could tell, Reiki was the only opportunity being presented to me at that time. I duly booked myself in, paid the deposit, and went on the course with June.

On the first day of the course, all twenty-seven of us were seated in rows when Reiki Master Jason strode in. I couldn't ignore my feeling of unease. As he scanned the room looking for signs of rebellion or unease in our body language, I consciously altered my body language from defensive to uncompromising. I sat up straight, placed my hands on both knees, and looked him straight in the eyes. I was here to learn and would not be fooled by mumbo jumbo.

That morning we were taught nothing in particular, merely that we have chakras that are energy centres. He wanted us to understand that Reiki was an energy to which you got attuned. Apart from sharing some examples where Reiki had produced healing, most of the lecture was about him.

I found the subject of chakras interesting because only a few weeks earlier, Iain had persuaded me to attend a workshop with the medium tarot reader I had first seen. In this workshop she explained that we had energy centres running along our spines that, when blocked, contributed to disease. I viewed this piece of information with my usual skepticism. If I had important energy centres running along my spine, wouldn't I know about it? The workshop was supposed to have taught me how to see people's auras. It had done nothing for me except plant information that would help me process some of the information in this Reiki workshop.

I did have one interesting experience at the medium's workshop. We were invited to relay messages that we were picking up from spirit. There was no instruction on how to pick anything up or what to expect. We were to just do it. To my surprise, Iain spoke up and said he could see a little boy running with a toy airplane. The medium asked if anyone could take the little boy in spirit. Everyone stared blankly. None of us could take this little boy. She asked Iain for the boy's name and he replied 'David.' It suddenly dawned on me that I had had an abortion six years earlier and this could well be that little boy.

No sooner had the thought popped into my head than the medium looked straight at me and said, "He's yours, isn't he? He's come to wish you a happy Mother's Day."

This did nothing to ease my guilt over the abortion. I suddenly felt like crying, which was something I could not allow myself to do in front of so many people.

Jason proceeded to tell us repeatedly that we didn't need to know anything about chakras because by the end of the course we could lay our hands on ourselves, our plants our food, people, or animals, and the energy would just flow. It was at about this stage in the course that I began to see things floating around the room. I closed my eyes and shook my head, thinking there must be something wrong with me. Try as I might, I couldn't dismiss the images of what I can only describe as capuchin monkey faces that seemed to move around behind Jason. At first I thought it was the pattern in the wallpaper, but then the same thing happened to the pattern in the carpet.

When the time came for our first attunement, we were divided into groups of seven and led into another room where we sat on chairs lined up in a row. Jason told us he would stand behind each one of us and do something over our heads. He would then walk to the front of each of us and place our hands in the prayer position and eventually blow the symbols through us. As he stood behind me, I felt a sensation in my tummy that was similar to the feeling you get when you drive over a bridge. When the attunement process was complete, we sat in the lecture room awaiting Jason's return. I began to shiver until my teeth started to chatter. When Jason came back into the room, he looked directly at me and said that some of us were feeling the power of the attunement more than others. He said it would be different for each of us.

That evening I returned home, convinced I had been fleeced of £180.00. I sat drinking a cup of coffee and the shivering finally subsided. I had a thought about wanting to get out of my body; I didn't like what I was experiencing. I got up and looked in the mirror. Yes, it was still me. Get out of my body! What was I thinking? You can't get out of your body! You're you, and that's it. I didn't want to go back the next day for the final attunements. Don't be silly, I told myself. You've already paid the £180. If nothing happens, at least you tried.

Something peculiar happened when I awoke the next morning. My little schipperke dog Emerald woke up as usual next to me in bed. As always, she yawned and looked at me so I would stroke her. When she turned to look at me, her expression changed to one of absolute horror. She began barking at me as though I was a stranger. When I spoke to her, she looked at me closely and then seemed to recognize me. I laughed and thought she must have had a bad dream.

I arrived at the Reiki seminar the next day and sat down in the same seat. Jason immediately apologized for not telling us to watch our dogs when we got home. The attunement apparently changes our energy fields and often dogs don't recognize their owners and attack them. This was what clinched it for me. I trusted Emerald and her unusual reaction. I finally conceded that I had an energy field and something must have happened to change it during the attunements.

At the end of the seminar we did what is called a Reiki share. We divided into groups of five, with one person lying on a treatment table and the other four placing their hands on him or her. Everyone had a turn at lying down. As we took turns moving around the table, we were invited to speak about what we had felt. Everyone turned to me and said that my hands were the hottest and they could really feel it from me. I was now thoroughly convinced. I wanted to go out and heal the world and tell everyone about this wonderful system of healing.

During the ensuing weeks after the attunements, I drank plenty of water and placed my hands on myself at every opportunity in an attempt to heal and stay healthy. I had many dogs and seized every opportunity to lay my hands on them, too. I had been told the more I used my Reiki, the stronger it would flow.

One of my dogs was a pointer named Abby. She had come to stay with me for retraining and in the beginning had proved to be a nightmare on four legs. During her retraining stay with me, she had managed to demolish a settee by pulling it bit-by-bit through the bars of the cage in which I had safely left her. When I put her in the dog's room at the side of the house (whenever I went to bed or left the house), she would bark continuously, stopping only because she had lost her voice. She would enter the kitchen at every opportunity, opening the fridge door and scoffing whatever she could find, even if it were frozen solid. She would then proceed to throw it up all over the house. I had to change all my square door handles to round ones, as she was able to open any door. Then it took her only half an hour to figure out the new round ones. The doors themselves were no problem either; she simply chewed a hole in them, if she failed to open them.

Abby's owners didn't want her back, so I kept her. She slept on my bed and accompanied me everywhere I went. Over the next couple of years, she gradually settled in and I could safely leave her by herself. Surprisingly, after I used the Reiki on her, she began re-exhibiting all her old bad habits. This puzzled me.

Jeanne Ames

I had become a regular visitor to bookstores. I was not happy with the healing information I had been given at the Reiki Seminar, and wanted to learn more. On one such visit, I picked up a book called 'Heal Your Life' written by a woman named Louise Hay. From this book I managed to deduce that certain diseases could be attributed to a person's attitudes or perceptions of life. I perceived that Abby was re-exhibiting some of her problems because I was healing her. I also found books that explained more about the chakras and their corresponding organs. I even discovered that some diseases could occur because of problems with certain chakras. Slowly I built up my knowledge of healing to encompass a much broader spectrum than what had been presented by the Reiki Master Jason.

About three weeks after the attunements, a huge cold sore appeared on my lip, the largest one I had ever had. My constant flu-like condition drained me of energy. I phoned Henry, the man Jason had left in charge of affairs in the UK. Henry told me this was quite normal after a Reiki attunement, and that it would heal in time. He suggested I attend the next Reiki share meeting to get some healing, which I did. It did nothing for me except draw attention to the fact that my hands were producing a very noticeable flow of energy. I spent the next three weeks after the share trying to heal myself. In the end, I stopped going to the Reiki shares and slowly began to recover.

By this time, I had met a girl named Sandra and we had become good friends. Lucy had moved away and Sandra and I began going to the psychic fairs together. Through the Reiki group I was introduced to a man named Jeremy, a spiritual teacher who gave readings. I booked a reading with him and he told me I was here to teach. He talked about a ring pass knot and mentioned that an Angel with a sword was standing at my side helping me. He went into detailed information about past lives I had had. I was eager to tell him about my Reiki. He looked at me and said I didn't need the symbols to heal. He told me he had seen energies go from one person's aura into another at a Reiki demonstration, and therefore he didn't consider it an informed or safe practice. I had no idea what to do with this information. Jeremy appeared to be rather strange, so I approached Henry about it. He told me that Reiki was self protecting; however, he would check with Jason to make sure.

Now, at that time, Jason visited the UK every so often, attuning many people to Reiki levels one, two, and three. At the time, it cost £6000 to do Masters, and several people were signed up for it. I was considered a bit of a nuisance and a troublemaker who didn't believe in Reiki. Darn right I didn't believe in it! My dad had taught me to always use common sense, and my common sense was telling me I didn't feel well. I had learned from books that we had an electromagnetic field, which is self-explanatory if you look at the words. The field is electric and magnetic, and as we all know when wiring a plug, negative flows to positive and vice versa. This is a simple law of physics. It only makes sense to apply that law to the interaction of electromagnetic fields between healer and recipient. As I learned more about chakras, I discovered each one was linked directly to an endocrine gland. If you were healing someone and did not clear your electromagnetic field of any unhealthy or dense energy, it would very likely end up in your own field and you would have to digest it. That was why I was feeling so ill after the Reiki shares. No one had cleared themselves after or in between sessions because no one had told them it was necessary to do so.

Jeremy gave me the bullets to fire into the people in my Reiki group, all of whom just happened to be his clients. He fell short of backing up what he had told me, however, because he feared he would lose income from these clients. After telling me I was part of the 'spiritual family' on earth and that I could ring him anytime, he quickly became evasive and elusive.

I had made some meditation tapes that I used when healing my children and friends. The idea for this had come during the first workshop I had attended with the medium. When I recorded my voiceover, I included music and turned the meditation into a journey. I introduced whales and dolphins and used tapes of their sounds.

It was around this time that Henry asked me if I would do a healing on him. (My 'hot hands' were well known in the Reiki group.) After I had introduced him to the tapes, he decided I was a good prospect on whom to offload all his difficult clients. On one occasion, I was sent to heal a hotel owner, who had been having treatment for a very arthritic ankle. When I arrived for the healing, he hobbled out to greet me. We went up to one of the rooms and he lay on the bed. I put my hands on his swollen ankle. He put the on the headphones and listened to the tape. When I had finished, he noticed a marked improvement in his ankle and booked another healing session for the following week.

In the meantime, an old acquaintance of mine had phoned to say his dog was ill. He said he didn't really believe in what I was doing, but couldn't afford the vet, who had refused to treat his dog anyway because of unpaid bills. I said I didn't know what I could do but that I would try. When I arrived at his flat, the dog looked very ill. She had acute infected mastitis. I put my hands on her teats and she went into a deep sleep. After about twenty minutes, I told him I had finished and that I didn't know what else I could do.

I heard nothing more for a week and then received a telephone call from a man who said he had heard about the dog I had healed. He asked if I could do the same for his back. I hadn't studied Reiki to earn a living, but the possibility was definitely opening up for me. I agreed to go to this man's house. Before long, he was lying on a futon on the floor and I was laying my hands on him. It suddenly occurred to me that I might be subjecting myself to danger. During this man's healing, I became aware that certain chakras were blocked. I had a sudden urge to place a crystal on the blockages to help clear them. Unfortunately, I hadn't brought any crystals with me.

By the time I had booked the second appointment with the man at the hotel, I had amassed some crystals, which I took with me and placed on the parts of his body and energy field I intuitively knew needed clearing. When the healing was over, he was almost pain free. He asked if I would like to use a small room in the hotel as a healing room free of charge in return for giving him healings. This cleared up the problem of going to strange men's houses.

In a very short period, I managed to build up quite a clientele; however, I was not satisfied with my healing power. I wanted people to *know* that something had happened, to feel the energy. As always, the universe was happy to oblige. All my clients suddenly disappeared and the man who owned the hotel was no longer satisfied with having just a pain-free ankle. He didn't want to face up to or look at any of his emotional stuff, let alone talk to me about it, but, at the same time, wanted the ankle returned to the way it was before he had injured it at the age of eighteen. I racked my brain for inspiration as to how I could become a better healer and do this for him. I never found the answer and eventually left the hotel. I later heard that the problems with his ankle eventually returned and he was contemplating surgery.

I had learned that complete healing occurs only when people address their attitudes about the 'dis-ease' within their life. I had tried to create a cure without fully understanding that healing is a joint venture; each person is responsible for contributing his or her own share of the work. I was willing to provide the highest, purest energy I could channel in order to heal his dis-ease, but he needed to look at himself and let go of the resentment and anger he felt.

While I was healing at the hotel, I began to attend classes run by Jeremy, the spiritual teacher. He taught us how to clear our energy fields using visualization or by taking cold showers. That summer, when I still felt dirty after a bath, I would go outside and put the hose over my head and let the cold water wash over me to clean my energy field. It became a daily ritual. I was careful to clear my energy before each healing and at the end of each day. Eventually, though, I found some flower essences that I could add to my bath to ensure I cleared my energy field at the end of each day. The cold showers became too much to bear.

By the time I left the hotel, I had undertaken Reiki Two and was now able to heal long distance. I found this to be a much more potent form of healing. With the hands-on approach, I had to rely on what we called the Heineken effect, i.e., reaching the parts that most needed healing. After taking Reiki Two, I was able to direct the energy through the crystal to exactly the point I wanted it to reach. More importantly, people could really feel it flowing; the fact that I wasn't touching them merely increased their belief that something was actually taking place.

What had I learned from this chapter of my life?
(1) There is a universal energy and I could feel it in my hands.
(2) It took a Reiki attunement to make me aware of this.
(3) Despite the fact that I was dealing with energy, i.e., an unseen force, it could have dramatic effects (negative and positive) on my health.
(4) More about chakras and the consequences of not clearing and cleaning your energy field the same way you would clean your physical body.
(5) The world is an unkind place full of strangers, even in a Reiki group.
(6) I had an amazing ability to heal others.
(7) Healing brings up old patterns of behaviour, old emotions that have lain buried for years.
(8) To use crystals to empower the flow of healing energy and clear blockages.
(9) Sound on meditation tapes could help induce deep states of consciousness and healing.
(10) I wanted to heal the world and teach it to sing.
What was the Universe trying to teach me?

All my learning thus far in the school of life was used at the Reiki seminar. Once again, I was amongst strangers in an education system I knew nothing about. (Familiar territory!) Keeping it simple and using common sense enabled me to find information on how to make healing simple, safe, reliable, and accurate. I didn't know it yet, but I still had a long way to go. The 'keep it simple' and 'common sense' rules Dad had taught me were about to take me on the journey of a lifetime.

CHAPTER 4

Expanding wisdom into understanding

I had taken second degree Reiki and no longer needed to place my hands on a person to introduce the healing energy. I had been given symbols for distant healing and used this system to heal even if a person were in the same room. I still intuitively placed crystals to enhance the healing process. Despite this, my life seemed to have ground to a halt again. No clients were arriving at my door to be healed, and my Reiki group had become somewhat hostile.

I had made friends with a woman named Dorothy, who was signed up for the £6000 Masters course and also attended Jeremy's courses. When she booked me to do some healings on her, I questioned her about clearing the energy field. This was subsequently relayed to Jason, the Reiki Master, who asked her if she really needed to receive healing from me, if she really needed the hassle.

Dorothy was an interesting case. She had been suffering the effects of ME (Chronic Fatigue Syndrome) for more than twenty years. On one occasion I brought Iain along with me to help during the healing. As the healing progressed, I began to see faces materializing over Dorothy's face. At the time I said nothing to Iain. It was only when we were travelling home in the car that he asked if I had seen the strange faces hovering over Dorothy's face. One of the faces was Egyptian-looking with heavy eye make-up. Iain described it to me exactly as I had seen it. I could only assume we were seeing something that Jeremy called a 'past life' coming off Dorothy, or at least an image of what she looked like in that life. I have seen this happen many times in my journey as a healer and have learned not to be distracted by it. I believe that what happens in this life affects an individual's health. I have never found looking into past life experiences helpful in my work, although I'm sure there are cases where knowledge of past life experience can assist the healing process.

I became so disenchanted with the whole Reiki phenomenon that I declared I was no longer a Reiki practitioner. I telephoned Henry and asked him to remove me from the mailing list. I had the distinct feeling that I needed to totally disassociate myself from the whole Reiki movement. When I telephoned Jeremy to inform him of my decision, he told me that at least it would force them to look at what they were doing. I couldn't help thinking that it might help them even more if he were to voice his concerns to them.

I had decided to work as a healer, but I didn't know which therapy I wanted to use as a format for my healing. I posed this as a question to the universe and, as usual, it responded by placing situations and opportunities on my path that I could choose or decline.

I found myself going to a certain shop three times in one week. I had once tried to help the owner, a woman named Anne, when she had had a serious cold for weeks on end. I had lent her a crystal necklace and suggested she wear it. She had always viewed me with great suspicion, but from then on always made a hasty retreat when I entered the shop. Later, during one of my infrequent visits, she had sought me out. She had handed the crystal necklace back to me and asked how much she owed me. When I replied that she didn't owe me anything, her wariness of me seemed to increase.

On this particular visit, Anne was walking with the help of two walking sticks. Previous experience had taught me not to offer help unless asked. When I visited her shop again later that same week, our eyes met and I could see her pain and misery.

"You know what I do," I said to her. "I'll try to help you if you want; however, it is up to you to request it. I'll not mention it again unless you ask."

Two days later I received a telephone call from Anne. She said she was so desperate she would try anything. When I arrived to do the healing on Anne, she told me a little bit about what she had been doing in the past year to try and heal her back. She had been X-rayed and had visited osteopaths and other therapists. In the end, the doctors offered to encase her lower body in a plaster cast to see if it would help ease her pain. If this worked, then it would be a good idea to fuse her vertebrae to reduce her pain. The plaster cast had done nothing to ease the pain. It was while she was in the plaster cast that I had offered to help.

When I began healing Anne, I wondered if my public declaration that I no longer wished to be associated with Reiki would do anything to reduce my healing powers. I still used the crystals, but not the symbols. I started the flow of healing energy by using a method that had popped into my head some weeks earlier.

Anne had five sessions of healing with me. On New Year's Eve of that year, she threw away her walking sticks and danced the night away, much to the astonishment of all the people who frequented her shop, not the least of whom was her husband. She began attending the bi-weekly healing groups I conducted. In these groups, I would lead a meditation and then talk about a particular subject. The meditations would always include a visual journey. Never did I have a preconception of what the journey would be; it would just materialize in my head. I tried to stick to a format during these meetings, but was unsuccessful. Even when I wrote a plan down on a piece of paper, I would end up very briefly covering what I had written and then be sidetracked, either by a question from a student or by words and subjects that just seemed to materialize in my head. The meditations had a very powerful effect on the people in the group. At the time, I didn't realize what a powerful healing effect they were also having on me.

It was at one of these groups that Anne told us about a very big secret she was carrying. Anne and I had talked at length during her healings, but she had never mentioned the guilt and sadness she was carrying. Everybody in the group was quiet and accepting of her. She came to a couple more sessions and then stopped coming. She told me she was a Catholic and did not know how the church would react to her attending my group meetings.

Shortly after this, her husband called to say he was in bed with a bad back. I went to visit him and performed a healing. The next day he was up and about again. A year later I was called to heal his back again. His manner and attitude made it very clear that I should not mention what Anne had disclosed to me. They had moved to my area to get away from gossip and recrimination, and some months later moved away for good.

I concluded that you can run but you can't hide from your emotional baggage. Only healing and correct counselling can eradicate the emotional cause of any dis-ease within your life.

I was still searching for a method of healing and a title I could use that people would recognize and draw people for treatment. I intended to use the skills I had already developed in conjunction with my chosen therapy. This search led me to take a course for colour healing, or chromo therapy. My friend Sandra had decided to enroll in the course and I eventually joined her. The course was over a two-year period, with one weekend every month spent in London. Money was tight, so we stayed with my friend Annette on our weekends in London.

Jeanne Ames

I learned about the science of colour on the chromo therapy course, which was based on the works of Ghadiali Dinshah. I found out that each shade of every colour has a specific chemical content. I learned there are lines in colour called Fraunhoffer lines, named after the scientist who discovered them. Our teacher had obtained the Dinshah family's permission to teach the course and use the information contained in Dinshah's books for the content of the course. She also employed a physics teacher, an acupuncturist, a counsellor, and a nurse who taught us anatomy and physiology, the basic groundwork for energy therapy.

During the counselling part of the course, I learned that I needed to change the way I interacted with people. I began to look at my aggressive stance to life. I learned to really listen to what people were saying (instead of forming my own opinion about what was being said) and to take action instead of reacting. The common sense regime I had always used seemed to be in alignment with the scientific portion of the course, where I learned how to introduce colour to different parts of the body to achieve a certain result. I learned that placing a film of coloured paper over a lamp and then directing the beam of the lamp to various parts of the human anatomy produced a specific frequency of colour that would achieve an expected result. It was not just a case of applying the hands and praying for results; it was specifically backed by scientific knowledge of frequency.

During the course, our teacher Fran had the use of a German colour-healing machine. Each one of us was given an opportunity to experience this machine. When I went to the therapy room for my session, Fran asked me what colour I would like. I told her I would leave it to her. She chose a peach colour. As I lay under the machine with the strobe light passing over my body, I began to feel lively and exhilarated. A Michael Jackson's song was belting out in my head. A plant on the windowsill caught my attention. As I looked at it, I heard it say, "Tell her to move me. I don't like it here. Too much red." By now I was accustomed to words materializing in my head, but I had never heard from a plant. When the session was complete, I gathered up enough courage to tell Fran what had occurred. She laughed and told me she had a nature spirit in her garden that sometimes came into the house, only to be chased out by her cat. The plant was moved. (Like Jeremy, Fran had the ability to see energies.)

One weekend during the chromo therapy course, I brought along the big crystal that I used for distant healings. One of the teachers in the course was an elderly nurse. She had completed her nurse's training but decided it wasn't enough, so had gone on to study reflexology, acupuncture, and chromo therapy. She was a diabetic and had problems with arthritis. That morning she looked very weary. During the lunch hour, I offered her a healing. By now I had found a way to introduce the specific chromo therapy frequencies I had been taught by using a crystal instead of a lamp and filter paper, but I had no way of knowing if it really worked. She accepted my offer of a healing, so I picked up my crystal and began the healing. As I began to introduce colour, she exclaimed. "Ooh, purple to my pancreas. Yes, that is just what I need." Each time I changed colours, she would describe what she saw and where I was sending it. I did not tell her what colours I was sending or where I was sending it. Now I had positive confirmation that the new healing system I had developed really worked!

This lady also taught me something else. Our homework one weekend was to specify a course of treatment for a heart problem. When it came time to do the homework, I did what I had done all my life and what many human beings do without realizing it: I tuned in to my intuition, or Higher Self, as I now refer to it. Instinctively, I could see three ways to go in terms of what colours I could use for a heart problem.

When I told this to the nurse, she replied, "Quite right, Jean. Heart problems can arise from a problem with the kidneys, liver, or thyroid. You are intuitively covering all aspects of the healing scenario required to bring about a positive healing response."

While I was pleased that the nurse had believed in and understood my ability to see something of which I had no prior knowledge, I took it in my stride. Having been a strange child all my life, this was just a variation of normal for me. I had learned to appreciate my abilities instead of fearing them, and merely wanted to use them in a positive way.

I completed the chromo therapy course and used the information I had learned on some clients. I discovered that the chromo therapy lamp was not as powerful as using crystals to send healing energy, so I began using the two together.

I was still reading my tarot cards regularly, waiting for a sign that Roger might return. I missed him very much. One night I went to bed and found myself talking back to the voices in my head. "I want to work on meeting up with Roger somehow so I can speak to him. In the morning I want to know that I have done it." What a strange thing to say, I told myself as I fell asleep.

I awoke the next morning having completely forgotten my affirmation the previous night. I proceeded with my day as usual. I let the dogs out in the yard, and cleaned and tidied the house. When I went to let the dogs in, I was horrified to discover that the gate was unlocked and they were missing. Having found her freedom, Abby had decided to take all the dogs for a walk.

In my panic, I asked the energies with whom I worked – that is, the voices in my head -- to please bring the dogs home safely. I jumped into my van and drove around the block looking for them, but to no avail. I went to the local shop and asked Anne if anyone had reported seeing some dogs running loose. On impulse, I picked up the local paper and paid for it. I got in my van and returned home to find the dogs waiting for me.

Relieved, I sat on the sofa and began reading the paper I had bought, something I didn't normally do. As I browsed through it, I came across my Horoscope. At the time, I was still of the mindset that 'shit happens and then you die.' I looked to my stars for some encouraging news that would help me face the day. As I read my Horoscope, the words seemed familiar. My immediate thought was that the shop had sold me yesterday's paper. I could very clearly remember having read the words before. I checked the date on the TV screen. No, it was definitely today's paper. Then I remembered the dream I had had that morning, during which I had read a paper I didn't normally purchase. I also remembered my affirmation of wanting to know that I had worked on meeting up with Roger during the night. Although I had no recollection of having met up with Roger, I was convinced that something had happened.

From then on, each night as I prepared for bed, I made an affirmation regarding what I wanted to work on in my life. I also taught Iain and Marie this principal, and they used it when sitting exams or going for interviews.

One day Iain came running into the house, exclaiming that he had lost his ferret down a rabbit warren. He wanted me to look into it and tell him where the ferret was. I told him I was unable to see anything and that he'd have to work on it. This meant that before he went to sleep he would need to make an affirmation to go out and find the ferret. "Okay, "he said. "I thought that was what you would say."

Three days later, when the missing ferret was all but forgotten, Iain was out for the evening in the local pub with his friend Toby. Upon nearing our house on the way home, Iain and Toby decided to have a race around the block in their cars. About two hundred yards from our house near my horses' field, Iain spotted what he thought was a rat coming out of the field. Having witnessed many of his pigeons being killed by rats, Iain decided to run it over. As he approached it, something made him stop. He got out of the car to investigate. It was his ferret!

What were the odds of Iain finding a ferret that had travelled two hundred yards from our house to the field? What were the odds of it leaving the field at the precise time Iain was racing his friend on a whim down that particular stretch of road?

What had I learned?

(1) My healing worked with or without symbols.

(2) A degree of scientific explanation can be applied to healing. The science of colour frequency opened up this avenue of understanding. It also took me to the physics section of the library where I found books about DNA.

(3) Anatomy and physiology knowledge is required if we are to acknowledge and empower our healing process. Our body is a tool by which we can unravel our emotional distress and find peace and balanced health. A car does not run properly if it is not properly serviced. The human body is no different. It needs the correct fuel, correct maintenance, and a destination to take it forward. If it is not correctly serviced, putting your foot on the throttle will only cause a breakdown.

(4) Plants communicate

(5) Nature spirits exist and animals can see them.

(6) My intuition is a valuable tool, always open to expansion, learning, and understanding.

(7) The thoughts I have when I go to bed create to a certain extent what I am working on while out of body during sleep. I can program myself to work on certain things. Even though I might not get exactly what I've asked for in the way I expected it, I know that a way will be shown to me.

(8) There are no coincidences; what you think on all levels creates the life you live.

What was the universe teaching me?

There are no coincidences. I am responsible for everything I create in my life, from the situation with my ex-husband to learning Reiki. The Earth is the University of the Soul. We come here to learn. The ring pass knot that Jeremy had mentioned is like an electric blanket around the earth. When we incarnate, we pass through it and all memories are wiped out. The human baby starts with its own DNA blueprint, already programmed. The only way to access any of this knowledge is by deep introspection, total openness and honesty with the self, and by always listening to the inner voice. It sometimes takes an illness to open us up to this unseen indefinable part of ourselves.

CHAPTER 5

Negatives

Going to see Jeremy for a reading introduced another aspect to the voices in my head. Jeremy, who could see energies very clearly, said he often came across someone who claimed to be a channel for Jesus or the archangel Michael. In reality, that person was channelling John Smith from Warwickshire, who having passed over and realizing he still existed, thought he could help someone "down here" find the truth. Perhaps he felt he never had a say during his last lifetime on earth, and now was going to have his say about everything.

I have already mentioned that I felt safe during the séances because the woman from the spiritual church said her guide would watch over us. Most people are wary of Ouija boards, and they should be. After ten years of research, I can see the reason why such negatives exist. The question of whether they are good or bad energies often arises. My reply is usually that the universe presents you with what you need for your learning. As infuriating and painful as this might seem, there is a reason for everything. Protective measures should always be taken before any process such as meditation, healing, chanting, or even day-to-day activities. If, however, there is something else for you to learn, then a 'negative' will inevitably find a way to manifest, no matter what precautions you take. There is no 'good,' 'bad,' 'negative,' -- only an opportunity to learn from each and every situation. After taking the right precautions before commencing meditation, healing, or channelling, I've found my best instrument of discernment is me. Gut instinct very rarely lets me down.

How do you recognize gut instinct versus your own mental fears? The more you tune into yourself and listen, the more definite and discernable the messages become. Just as a baby learns to talk slowly and with difficulty at first, you must learn the language and recognize the words and the way in which your sixth sense serves you. A good place to start is by spending time in nature. Go out in a field or park and find a large tree. Sit and look at something non-human, like the sky or a plant. The dialogue will begin without fail. Sixth sense is something we all possess. It's an unseen, intangible part of us that is very often undervalued and underused. How often do we take time to just sit and be? The opportunity to listen to ourselves arises only if we take the time to create that opportunity.

By the time I saw Rosamund the tarot reader for the third time, I had already begun doing what she had told me to do, which was to heal others. When I had asked her how I should do that, she had said "Just go out and heal." My gut instinct was my only guide. There were many places I could have gone in my search for a way to become a healer. In the end, I created my journey, and the universe obliged by placing the opportunities for learning right in front of me. It never occurred to me there might be books on such a weird subject. In fact, previous experience had taught me it wasn't wise to pursue this avenue.

I began to run what I called 'crystal parties,' where I would do tarot readings and bring a few crystals to sell. On one occasion I met a woman who said she needed healing and asked if I would do some crystal healing on her. This was before I had received my Reiki attunements or knew very much about healing. In sheer desperation I had often put my hands on sick cats or dogs and tried to heal them, but nothing had ever happened. Now that I knew about the crystals, I thought perhaps this was what Rosamund had meant when she had said "Go out and heal."

When I arrived at the woman's house, I had no idea what I was going to do or how I would do it. I just pointed the crystal and followed my instinct. She exclaimed that she could see a green light coming from the crystal in my hands. From this information, I created the belief that it was actually the crystal that was doing the healing. After about twenty minutes of performing maneuvers that seemed appropriate under the circumstances, I left and thought no more about the healing or the woman.

After a few days I became extremely unwell. My eyes were swollen, itchy and red. The skin on my face was very blotchy and irritated. I looked dreadful. Three weeks later I went into Norwich to find something to soothe my skin. A woman approached me while I was buying cream in a shop. To my surprise, it was the woman on whom I had performed the healing. She proceeded to tell me how much better she felt. She had been in hospital to have a cataract operation and had had an allergic reaction to the antibiotics they had used. Her eyes had become puffy and red and her skin blotchy. Having gotten over her problems, she was now out shopping. I couldn't help but compare what had happened to her with the state of my own health.

My skin and eyes were an exact mirror of what had happened to her, the only difference being she had recovered and I was still suffering. Fortunately, after another week, all my symptoms disappeared and the creams were thrown away.

A couple of weeks after recovering, I attended the workshop where I first learned about chakras. As I moved from one room to another during one of the breaks, I came across the medium Rosamund coming down the stairs. I seized the opportunity to tell her about my constant weariness. She took my right hand and opened it to inspect the palm. After suppressing a gasp, she took three steps backwards up the stairs away from me. She pointed to a line in my palm and said that I had a negative attachment that was having a seriously adverse effect on my liver.

"What do I do about it?" I asked.

She said she would put me on her protection list. For some reason, that didn't inspire a lot of confidence in me. This information would probably be enough to send most people into complete denial of anything energetic, esoteric or spiritual, but I still believed that common sense would show me the way.

The Universe did show me the way. I attended Jeremy's workshops just long enough to learn how to unhook attachments and clear the energy field. It would have been so much easier if Rosamund herself had just qualified what she told me and given me some advice or a simple exercise to do.

I had another similar experience with an attachment. A great many people were interested in my 'hot hands,' not the least of whom was a certain yoga teacher named Debbie. I was invited to sit in on a Reiki workshop run by her Reiki Master, who had come down from Wales. While this Reiki Master was talking about Reiki and how it originated, she kept referring to framed photos of Usui, Hayashi, and Takata. I kept hearing 'idolatry' in my head and was uncomfortable with the way this woman was teaching. She said she had experienced a warm flow of energy, but could not cite any specific case histories. Then she asked me to share my experiences, since I had taken my first-degree attunements. I found myself excitedly relaying the story of the man who owned the hotel where the seminar happened to be taking place. I thought the response would be wonderful. Instead, I sensed a discomfort in both the Reiki Master and Debbie, who both immediately stated they had never experienced such things and they should not be expected. I felt a surge of rejection and frustration. Like my mum, they ignored what could be, were afraid of the unseen and didn't believe in miracles.

Eager for someone to share my experience and to show her what she was missing, I offered Debbie a healing. She seized the opportunity. We went to the room in the hotel where I could work free of charge. I used the same procedure on her as I did with everyone else. I put on the meditation tape, gave her earphones, and did the healing. Since she was a Reiki Second Degree, I was anxious for her reaction to what I had done, what I had created in the healing.

"What did you think of the tape?" I asked her. "I had never done meditation before and I just put it together."

To my great surprise, she snapped back at me angrily. The force of her anger was enough to halt me in my tracks. All the old patterns of being afraid to open up about what I saw or knew came rushing to the surface. She left rather hurriedly, but not before telling me that my meditation had reminded her of some re-birthing she had done when she had remembered a past life, an incident that had upset her at the time. I had obviously touched a sore spot.

Two days later I had a very strange dream. I had felt very uncomfortable for two days after performing the healing on Debbie, and found myself constantly under the hose in the garden trying to clear my energy field. In the dream, I got into a shower after a series of frightening events, however, the shower had a wooden floor and the cold water had nowhere to run. I just couldn't get rid of what it was that was making me uncomfortable.

In desperation, I rang Jeremy.

"Hang on," he said. "Let me look at your energy field."

Just let him do his thing, I told myself. He's a bit strange, after all. I told him about Debbie's healing and her reaction to my tape.

"She's angry with you," he replied. "She is so angry she has hooked into you on the astral plane. Just unhook it. You know how to do that, don't you?"

"What?" I replied. "I have no idea how to do that."

"Don't worry," he said. "I'll do it for you."

Later, at one of his classes, I learned the simple technique for unhooking. I wondered why he hadn't told me what to do over the phone. My naivety left me feeling susceptible, vulnerable, and angry. I didn't like feeling vulnerable, especially after what I had experienced with my ex-husband.

I was angry that Debbie, an established Reiki practitioner, had hooked into me. She should have known what she was doing. This was completely new territory to me. I phoned her and told her about my dream and my conversation with Jeremy (whom she disliked) and how he had unhooked her from me.

"Well, I never!" she exclaimed. "I was in the kitchen and suddenly exploded in anger for no reason."

When we checked the time of her explosion, it would have been about the same time Jeremy had unhooked her from me. She was totally amazed, completely unaware of any hooks or even the existence of such things. You might think this little bit of information would have inspired Debbie to seek some guidance from Jeremy, but she never did.

I was able to accept that something had indeed happened, albeit unseen and distance-related. There was far more to this energy stuff than met the eye. It could be dangerous, I thought. This stirred a distant memory of something Rosamund had said during one of my tarot readings.

"It's like putting your finger into a live electricity socket when you begin working with this stuff," she had said, shaking her head ominously.

No explanation was offered, as I had run out of time for the reading. I made a mental note never to leave any of my future students or clients in such a place. That was the signal for the Universe to create even more opportunities for learning.

I knew I wanted to continue being a healer and find out as much as I could about the entire subject. I also wanted to learn how to do it safely. It was imperative that anyone I healed receive the best possible healing and self-empowerment. At the end of each healing session, I taught each person how to unhook attachments and clear their energy fields.

Not long after I had publicly declared that I no longer wished to be associated with Reiki, Jeremy phoned me. He had received an enquiry from a woman about her dog that had paralyzed hind legs. I was the only animal healer he knew. I arranged to see Thomas, a nine-month-old red setter. When I began the healing, Thomas was dragging himself in circles around the room. As I proceeded, he began to calm down and his circles would deviate every time he entered the crystal's energy field. It was as though he could see the beam of energy; to him it was as real as any solid object. Eventually he fell over and drifted into a deep sleep. His owner booked me for five more sessions. I learned that Thomas had had a scan of his spine and his vets had recommended euthanasia. They also wanted to do a brain scan that would have cost his owner Christine another £800, which she could ill afford.

Jeanne Ames

After five sessions of healing, Thomas was fully recovered. Seven years later, he was still alive and walking on all four legs. When the vet in charge of Thomas asked to meet me, of course I was eager to do so. The vet was supposed to come and meet me at a talk I had arranged with some of Christine's friends. He never showed up, but passed on another client to me. Unfortunately I wasn't able to facilitate a miracle with their dog Spirit; however, Spirit's owners did write and thank me for the extra time they had to say goodbye and come to terms with his death.

During the talk I gave to Christine's friends, I shared what I had learned about working on intentions during sleep. As usual, the people I was addressing were unfamiliar with alternative forms healing, meditation, mediums, etc., and I faced a sea of crossed arms and legs. They had heard about Thomas the dog, and I had taken Anne along with me; however, they still remained unconvinced.

Some years later, when I was at Christine's shop, a woman came up to me and said, "You saved me money on my telephone bill, you know." Now, I had seen and done some pretty amazing things but this was a new one for me. "Yes, she continued. "Every time I want to talk to my daughter who lives a long-distance phone call away, I go out and work on it the night before and she always rings me the next day."

This was also around the time that the voices in my head began telling me their names; Paul the Venetian and Hilarion were two of them. At that time I was into Arab horses and was searching for an appropriate mate for my mare Velvet. Thinking the voices in my head were trying to suggest stallions I should use, I would say, "No, I don't like such and such a stallion," or "Indeed, that one. Thank you!"

I came to learn that the group of energies with whom I worked was called the Masters of Wisdom. In my five years of practice and development as a healer, not once did I ever come across a healer who acknowledged or recognized this group. None of the healing books I had read mentioned the Masters of Wisdom; however, I did come across a book by Alice A. Bailey called White Magic, which I instinctively bought. Although the book intrigued me, I found it quite complicated and difficult to understand. The information I did glean from it, however, I found very useful. When I read a book, I never read from page to page. Instead, I skip pages, sometimes reading only four pages out of an entire book. I know there will be something for me to learn on one of those pages.

Darkness is only Light not Switched On

During my healing stint at the hotel, we decided to hold a 'healing day.' Many of the local practitioners were invited. Many people who had heard of my success with the owners showed up. As I wandered around the various stalls, I came across a woman selling flower essences. I picked up a leaflet about Australian Bush Flower essences. One essence immediately caught my eye; the word 'protection' leaped out at me from the description of its properties.

I moved on and a man named Bill came over and introduced himself to me. Although he had attended the first Reiki seminar with me, I didn't remember him. He told me he had attended a course on the Australian Bush Flower essences and that he would make me up the Fringed Violet essence and mail it to me. I gave him my address and the essence duly arrived. Bill became a friend and started attending my bi-weekly groups. He was a practitioner who used a form of healing using sound waves and a computer. We became friends and conversed on the phone most mornings.

About a year later, Bill came across something known as birth frequency healing and attended a course on it. He modified what he had learned to enable him to pass the birth frequency through his computer and introduce it to a recipient's energy field. He offered me the chance to try it. I was always looking to heal myself further and create balance within my physical body so I could channel the highest possible frequencies, so I eagerly accepted the offer.

What had I learned?
(1) It was possible for my decision-making and my moods to be influenced by something I couldn't physically see.
(2) Safe, simple ways to ensure the only decision-making influence in my life was me.
(3) You definitely cannot trust other people to help you in the same way your family helps you. Rosamund had given me enough information to frighten the living daylights out of me when she offered to put me on her protection list. Jeremy had helped me, even though a few extra minutes on the phone would have taught me how to do it myself. Instead, I left the conversation feeling unempowered and dependent.
(4) Common sense told me that if you were 'picking up' frequencies -- much the same as a radio transmits music -- it is important to have some knowledge and discernment about the "people" with whom you are dealing. My natural distrust of anything outside of family, as taught by my parents, was serving me well in this instance.

(5) Clearing and cleansing the energy field daily and being aware of how you are functioning on an energy level are necessary to eradicate interference. It is important to establish an inner knowledge for your communicating process. Once you have established, beyond all doubt and with your deepest gut instinct, that what you are dealing with is positively trying to help you, teach you, or enhance your life, tell no one the signs given before each communication. The positive entity you are working with will give you signs in a frequency that only you will recognize. It is a special language between you and your angel, an unwritten code by which you will know exactly what and who you are dealing with. You can devise your own way of interpreting what is said. For instance, I learned to use the language of colour and animal totems in my communication process. Each individual partnership between an Angel and a human being will have a different approach and format based on that person's experience in his or her life at the time. A request to the Universe will always bring a reply. The Angels cannot help if you do not specifically ask thereby giving them permission to help. This is the law of free will in actuality.

What was the universe teaching me?

I had choices regarding discernment; I could choose who I wanted to listen to. Situations had arisen which confirmed my belief that you can program yourself to work on certain aspects of your life while out of body during sleep. I could choose to continue on the path of a healer if I wished, bearing in mind that help and advice was not readily available. Looking back at my school days, I was well prepared for such an adventure. I had been provided with ample experiences for coping with the circumstances in which I found myself.

One such circumstance was when I was asked to heal a young woman's grandfather, who was eighty-three and had bone cancer. It was obvious to everyone but the granddaughter that he was ready to die. I agreed to do the healing and travelled to Ipswich to carry it out, having no idea how or what I was going to do or say to this man. When I arrived, he was sitting in a chair looking pale, yellow, sullen, and angry. I began the healing, struggling to find a way to help him with his passing; it was obvious he wanted to go.

The only thing I could think of that might help him was to prepare him for the journey. But how? I desperately searched for a way to convey what I needed to say. As usual, help arrived. I swallowed hard as the thoughts came into my head. He was an extremely grumpy individual and I didn't want to upset him. Somehow I found myself talking about what happens after death.

I described what I had heard and believed, which was that those who have no prior understanding of life after death are taken to a hospital scenario, which they can accept because it is what they know.

Before I could go any further, the old man's eyes lit up. "I know," he said. "I've been there. When I was six, I was an extremely sickly child. I was in hospital with pneumonia. I died while my mum was at my bedside. I slipped out of my body through an open window and straight into the hospital you just mentioned. I wanted to stay, but I heard my mum cry out in anguish. I couldn't do that to her, so I went back. They only gave me until the age of twelve to live, you know. I didn't do so bad making it to eighty-three." Then he looked at me and said, "I've been all around the world, you know, yet I've never been on an airplane or a ship."

I knew he was talking about astral travel. We were fellow journeyers who had stayed silent to appear normal. The twinkle in his eye told me my job was done. I finished up and left a much less grumpy old man.

CHAPTER 6

Birth Frequency Healing and Flower Essences

By this time, I knew that a healer must first 'heal thyself.' Simple logic had told me that if I were channelling healing energy through a crystal to heal another person or animal, I would also be a recipient of the healing frequencies. Much like the fuse in a plug that safeguards an electrical circuit, this healing energy frequency had to pass through me.

Since beginning my journey as a healer, I had experienced several vivid dreams. Although the dreams were never straightforward, they were always communicated in words similar to those I heard in my head from what I now know to be the Masters of Wisdom.

One of my dreams seemed to indicate that I should do Reiki Masters.

"No way!" I declared out loud. "I'm not going down that road again. Besides, I can't afford it."

The voices and the feeling of being drawn to seek Master's attunements persisted for a couple of months. Finally I relented and stated that I would do Masters only if I found someone to give it to me for £600.00.

At the very first Reiki talk by Reiki Master Jason, I had met a large, boisterous woman named Doris, who I instantly disliked. Her manner was very aggressive and she wore a huge necklace of amber with a massive quartz crystal in it. I made a mental note to steer well clear of her, but our paths had crossed a few times over the ensuing years. From mutual contacts I learned that she had completed her Reiki one, two, and Masters rather inexpensively.

A couple of months later, after ignoring my gut instinct about the Reiki Masters, I was clearing out a drawer and came across a leaflet about Reiki from Doris. Before I knew it, I was dialing her number. No harm in enquiring, I thought. I probably won't do it; I'm just enquiring. She would never give it to me for six hundred pounds, I told myself

After I enquired about the price of doing Masters, Doris told me what the cost of 3a would be, considering I was only a second degree. Now, my

Dad had impressed upon me the pitfalls of being a 'bighead,' as he called it. Years of this advice had caused me to be very quiet when it came to my attributes. I considered anyone who spoke out about their attributes to be arrogant and bigheaded. I was well aware of my abilities, but kept them secret and never proclaimed them in a positive way out loud. This would have made me one of those big heads my dad had always said was heading for a fall. (Little did I know that I was about to meet two Australians who would change all this. The universe would address my needs again! It is only through writing this book that I am now able to recognize and appreciate all the experiences in my life and understand how they have transformed me into the woman I am today.)

I was rather surprised when I found myself interrupting Doris and telling her about the healings on Anne and Thomas and that I didn't think I needed to do 3a. All I wanted was the Masters attunement so I could begin teaching what I knew under the heading of 'Reiki.' She insisted on sending me a leaflet containing her price list and what each level entailed in terms of instruction, which I duly received and threw in the garbage.

"There!" I told my Angels. "It's £600 for 3a and £800 for Masters. Oh well, I tried."

A week later I received an unexpected telephone call from Doris. She had thought about what I had said and decided to give me the attunements for £600.00. I remembered that my friends Sandra and Bill had offered to pay £200.00 each as their share of the cost of the of the Masters attunements. In return, I would give them the attunements up to Masters once I had become a Reiki Master myself. This appeared to be the perfect opportunity for me to find a 'heading' under which I could perform and teach my own form of healing, which included my technique of using colour. What was more, I could teach the use of colour safely and wisely in a two-day course; students wouldn't have to study for two years to use the chromo therapy lamp, as I had done.

The following week, I took the attunements from Doris over the course of two days. We agreed that she would give me only the attunements and not teach me her course for Masters. In between attunements, we chatted. She told me that some people had not paid her fees, even when she had given them time to pay. It struck me that Doris was one very angry lady. It could just as easily have been me sitting there relating all the situations in which people had treated me badly, but instead, I took it as an opportunity to use the counselling skills I had learned on the chromo therapy course. I was always being presented with opportunities to practice and learn my skills as a healer, to observe in others what I was trying to change about myself.

Two days after taking the Reiki attunements, I attended a workshop run by Iain White, the originator of the Australian Bush Flower essences. I experienced some powerful reactions to these essences, as well as some amazing results. The first one I used was an essence called Fringed Violet, which was supposed to protect your energy field. It certainly seemed to help me. At the workshop I learned a bit about the endocrine system and how to make up essences for others. I thoroughly enjoyed the entire two days and learned much that would help me receive the kind of responses I wanted during healings. I nurtured my clients with the same fervour my parents had nurtured me. I took it upon myself to affect the healing, despite any lethargy they might display about their emotional healing. As a child, I had been taught that when in distress you support unstintingly, and I did.

Khan, my old Doberman, suddenly developed swelling on either side of his throat and I took him to the vet.

"Lymphatic cancer," she pronounced. "I'm afraid the only thing you can do is have him put down, quite frankly the sooner the better."

"Oh, no!" I protested. "I'm going to take him home, at least for a couple of days."

Khan and I went home. The poor old boy had been very wobbly on his hind legs for quite some time, I told myself, trying not to let him see my distress. When I had been beaten by my ex-husband and had collapsed in a heap of tears in the aftermath, Khan had always been there to lick my face and give comfort in any way he could. We sat on the sofa together. I pressed my hands on him, willing the healing energy to flow and make everything alright, not thinking for a moment that this was even possible. For the next two days, all I did was sit with my hands on Khan. I also consulted the book Iain White had written and made up an essence containing all the Flower Essences he recommended for cancer. By the third day, Khan's lumps had disappeared and his legs were no longer wobbly. In fact, he came out for a walk for the first time in ages and made it around an eight-acre field!

Although relieved, I was still concerned that I might be missing something. He might still be in pain from this cancer; the fact that I couldn't see it didn't mean it was gone. I took him back to the vet. Her surprise was evident when she looked at him and felt all around his throat where the lumps had been. She moved to his rear and felt his lymph nodes, trying to find signs of lumps. As she stood there lost for words, I felt the need to explain to her that I was a healer and had spent two days healing him after her diagnosis. I can only describe her reaction as one of fear. She rushed me out of the examining room, telling me I didn't need to bring him back and if I needed any medication for his arthritis all I had to do was call for a prescription. Khan lived for another two years and died of natural causes. I didn't have to have him put down.

With Khan's recovery in mind, I decided I would take some essences to help lower my blood pressure, which had been a problem for me ever since giving birth to Iain and Marie. The medication I was on had made me feel so ill I had stopped taking it. I felt I had no quality of life, and despite several changes in medication, nothing seemed to work well for me.

I again consulted Ian White's book and made up an essence containing all the ones suggested for blood pressure. Within a day, my arms had broken out in an eczema rash as bad as it had been in the past. This jogged my memory. When working in the Fish and Chip shop, my eczema had been so unsightly my boss had asked if there was anything I could do to improve the look of my hands and arms. I had tried creams, changed soaps, and eliminated soaps, all to no avail. Then my ex-husband was put in prison for a year. Because I had become accustomed to living my life on automatic pilot, surviving from day to day, trying not to remember my painful past, always with my ears tuned for a strange car coming in the drive that would signal a usually troublesome visit from my ex husband, I didn't realize that the eczema had vanished a few days after he went to prison, when for the first time in a very long while I felt safe. The eczema had disappeared and I had not even noticed that it had miraculously disappeared in conjunction with my husband being jailed. The eczema outbreak which coincided with my taking the essence for blood pressure lasted only a few days and I was able to heal myself because I realized I was now in control and no one could ever put me in that position again unless I allowed it. A deeply buried memory had come to the surface and been dealt with in a balanced way with wisdom and understanding.

At that point I was attending as many spiritual meetings run by Jeremy and Rosamund, the medium and tarot reader, as I could. At some point during each one of these meetings, someone would always mention that I appeared to be angry. I had been trying for some time to balance my aggressive stance and it never ceased to infuriate me that these people felt the need to point it out to me.

In one of my books on flower essences, I came across an Alaskan flower essence called Blue Elf Viola, which would supposedly 'help you find the seeds of your anger.' Surely that would do the trick, I thought. I purchased the essence and duly made myself up a bottle. For two weeks I felt like a caged tiger, as I began to acknowledge my anger. At one of the spiritual meetings I attended, an acquaintance greeted me and asked how I was doing. I told her I felt very angry but didn't know why.

Several days later, I watched the film 'Free Willy' about the Killer Whale on TV. As usual, my body jerked tearfully when I tried to suppress my tears during the sad parts. The little boy in the film was being fostered and was angry and upset at life in general. It struck a deep chord within me. Then a strange feeling came over me. I felt like I was in a trance. I heard my dad say to Mum, "Don't worry, love. It'll be okay this time." It felt like I was in the womb listening and understanding what my parents were saying. I immediately understood the seed of my anger. For the first time, I had the experience of knowing something and seeing the bigger picture in the same split second! It was part of the language that my Angels used to communicate and which they were now developing within me.

Several years before I was born, Mum had given birth to a son named Michael. At birth he appeared to be a healthy baby; however, when he was two days old, he suddenly turned blue and was rushed to hospital where he died. Mum never saw him again after he was taken from her. From that day forward, she had a crippling fear of doctors, hospitals, and ambulances. Michael had been born with a hole in his heart. There was nothing they could have done for him, she told me. The doctors told her and my father that history was not likely to repeat itself, and after a short break they could try again for another child. Within months, Mum's periods had stopped again and her abdomen began to swell. She was pregnant. In those days there was no such thing as a pregnancy testing kit or ultrasound. As far as she was concerned, her body was telling her she was pregnant. When the pregnancy reached the six-month stage, the doctors became increasingly worried. Repeated examinations failed to find any trace of a baby, a situation belied only by the size of her expanding abdomen. Eventually a specialist was called in. As he examined Mum, a fountain of blood shot up the wall and all over the bed. She had experienced a phantom pregnancy.

When Mum finally did become pregnant with me, she feared the future would be a repeat of past events. All throughout my life, I had always had an innate fear of the future. Every time I picked up the post or answered the phone, I expected to receive bad news. I could now see that this trait, this mental programming, had originated in the womb. Most humans and many animals use anger to camouflage fear. I had recalled the cellular memory of what Dad had said repeatedly to Mum in an attempt to allay her fears over her pregnancy with me. Wow! Those essences were good!

By that time, I also knew that anger was stored in the liver and gallbladder, fear in the kidneys, and so on. I began to pay attention to my fears, and created little mental exercises to remove them from my programming. By 'programming' I mean that I had been conditioned to respond to all circumstances in my life based on previous experience and learning. At the time, it was a revelation to me that my programming had begun in my mother's womb. Without the help of the flower essences and the angels that were assisting me, I would never have uncovered that part of me.

When I talk about 'skilled counselling,' I am referring to counselling by someone who understands how these patterns can arise and cause discomfort and eventually disease. Counselling to accomplish healing without this knowledge and understanding is the equivalent of trying to find your way out of the world's largest maze. There is a way out, but on the way to the exit many new compensating paths and programmes in the form of conditioned response are put in place. All these must be deleted in order to create balance. To achieve balance, care must be taken to not simply substitute one attitude or behaviour for another equally unbalancing behaviour pattern.

It was around this time that my friend Warren introduced me to a couple of Australians. Always suspicious of strangers, I made polite conversation with the girl named Natalie, who feigned an interest in my healing. I could tell she was equally wary of me. Her partner was a forthright, outspoken Australian named Adam. They had just moved to Norfolk to work for Warren. I left her my telephone number and offered to pick her up and take her to one of my group sessions. I heard nothing from her for a couple of weeks, and taught my first Reiki workshop before we met again.

The workshop went very smoothly and I was pleased with the results. I'll never forget seeing the light in the eyes of my students as they left to go out and unleash their healing on the world. The day after the workshop, I heard a new voice in my head, a much clearer and more commanding voice than I had ever heard before. It told me to get pen and paper, which I did. The communicator commended me on my workshop the previous day and used words that I had to look up in the dictionary. I wrote down what was said, and as the energy signed off, I looked for the name, thinking it would be one of my regulars. I was surprised when the reply was 'Kuthumi.' I had never come across this name before. I saw Doris a couple of days later and mentioned what had occurred. She told me she had come across the name in some Aura Soma bottles, although she had no idea what it was. .

It was around this time that Nat, as I would eventually call her, phoned and asked me to pick her up for the next group session I was conducting. I was relieved she was coming to that meeting alone, as I wasn't very comfortable with her extremely macho boyfriend. As we travelled to the meeting, she asked me what I had done the previous week. I told her about the Reiki workshop I had conducted and the channelling I had received from the new energy.

"Oh, my God!" she exclaimed. "I've got the shudders."

Sure enough, she was covered in goose bumps and shuddering uncontrollably.

"Just before we left Australia," she continued, "I saw a channelling of Kuthumi on a video. He was talking about opening light centres all over the world. What a coincidence because that is what Warren wants to do with the place he has just bought." (The extremely dilapidated mansion sat on 80 acres of overgrown, untended woodland.)

By the end of the evening I had decided I liked Natalie enough to tolerate Adam, although he appeared quite arrogant when he came to the next group meeting. I ran the group as usual. When everybody had come out of the meditation, I went around to each person, asking if they wanted to share anything with the group. Several had seen a particular animal and I was able to provide some insight as to what the animal might mean in terms of their learning. When I came to Adam, he struggled to find words, but nothing seemed to come. He huffed and puffed. Nat broke into a fit of giggles, saying it was the first time she had ever seen him speechless. The only words he could muster were "I'm a basket case."

On the way home, Adam said he had never experienced anything so powerful in a meditation or workshop. I was pleased that my skills in leading meditation and facilitating an energy exchange had impressed someone like him. Nat and Adam lived just down the road from me. I became a regular visitor and our friendship grew.

Eventually Nat, Adam, Warren and his wife Jill all took Reiki one with me. It was only my second workshop, so it scared me a little when Adam and Nat seemed to leave their bodies for up to fifteen minutes after I had completed the attunement process for each of them. Standing in front of what seemed to be an empty shell of a body for up to fifteen minutes was somewhat unnerving, to say the least. If they didn't return to their physical bodies, how would I explain it to the authorities?

Nat, Adam, and I became close friends. Adam became the brother I never had. Natalie had a degree in psychology and would often question me about my behaviour patterns or use of words, which helped me see how I was ticking mentally and emotionally. She was the first person to question me in years. I learned more about myself in the safe space of the friendship and trust that existed between us.

Nat and Adam moved to London, but always kept in regular touch. One day Nat rang me to say that Adam had proposed. After overcoming her initial fear of commitment and responsibility, she had accepted. The date for the London wedding was set and they wanted me to attend. When Dad had been alive, I had travelled fearlessly anywhere I wanted to go. I knew that if I had ever gotten lost he would have come to my rescue no matter where I was. Since his death, though, I had retreated into my shell and had ventured no further than the outskirts of Norwich. When I made the excuse that I couldn't afford the train ticket to London, Natalie offered to pay for it. I then made the choice to go.

I had been to Liverpool Street on numerous occasions on my own to meet Dad when he worked in London. Now I had what appeared to be an uncontrollable fear of travelling. Upon arriving at Norwich train station, I scanned the arrivals and departures list for Liverpool Street, knowing the train was due to leave soon. I spotted a train heading for Liverpool on platform 4 and figured they had just left the 'ST' off the title. The train filled up with an unusual amount of Asians. It also seemed to be somewhat of a luxury train. Must have changed since I last came, I told myself. Eventually I plucked up enough courage to ask the man sitting next to me if the train was going to Liverpool Street. He laughed and replied, "No Liverpool." The doors were already shut and the guard had blown his whistle as I made my swift exit. I hurriedly asked which platform was for Liverpool Street and was pointed in the direction of a train about to leave.

I made the journey to London without further incident. Sharon, another Australian friend, met me at Liverpool Street to show me the way to Natalie and Adam's house. I made a mental note never to travel again unless absolutely necessary. (Little did I know what the Universe had in store for me!)

Several months later, my friend Sharon announced she was going home to Australia. I was sad. I liked my Aussie friends with their "out there" attitudes and tacit acceptance of me and what I knew. They were never bothered by my uncanny ability to know what they were thinking. My confidence in voicing what I had learned to silence as a child had grown because of the time I had spent with them.

I went with Nat and Adam to look at Staffordshire bull terrier pups. In true Jeannie fashion, as the litter of ten pups swarmed round us, one immediately caught my eye.

"Is that our pup?" Nat asked as I picked up the pup.

"No, this one is mine." I then proceeded to go through the rest to pick out a pup for them.

Iain was on holiday at the time and came home to Sass, the new addition to our household. Iain had owned a Staffie that we had witnessed being run over and had brought home with us. After some healing and tender loving care, we had named her Bess. Unfortunately, Bess was killed in a fight with Blitz, my German shepherd. Iain was distraught at her loss. He and Marie had both bought Jack Russell terriers soon afterwards, although nothing could ever replace Bess.

Prior to buying the new Staffie, I had had a dream in which I was trying to find Bess. I informed a big brindle male Staffie that appeared in the dream that I was definitely not taking him home. Later on in the dream, I was walking though a typical English council estate and the brindle dog appeared again.

When we arrived to view the litter from which Nat and Adam would eventually choose Jeannie (the name they gave her, much to the consternation of their parents in Australia who I think thought they had joined some kind of cult that was keeping them in England), I remembered the dream. As in the dream, a huge brindle Staffie dog came out to greet us. He was the father of the pups.

Adam and Nat eventually moved back to Norwich where we enjoyed many excursions to the beach with Jeannie and Sass. Their house, which was not far from where I lived, was big enough for me to conduct workshops. They had both progressed through the attunement process to level 3a.

It was around this time that Marie introduced Iain to Catherine, a friend from college, and they began dating. As it turned out, her mum, Wallis, had taken one of my horses on what is called 'meat for manners' some years previously. They both had horses. Wallis` horse Warrior was prone to breathing difficulties. After teaching Wallis a few techniques for clearing herself before riding him, his condition improved. I also made up some flower essences for him.

Wallis and Catherine began attending my bi-weekly groups with Iain, and brought along another friend named Bev. We nicknamed them 'The Three Musketeers.' The three musketeers informed me they would all like to take Reiki one. My friend Warren gave me the use of the orangery at his mansion to conduct the workshop.

Just before the workshop, my lodger Arron was rushed into hospital suffering from terrible stomach pains. He was diagnosed with a bleeding peptic ulcer. He spent a week in hospital and came home with some medication, which he took until all the pills were gone. When Arron arrived home from hospital, I had immediately consulted Iain White's Flower Essence book and put him on the remedies I thought were appropriate. In addition, I had done some healing on him.

Some weeks later, I took him for his follow-up appointment. A very worried looking Arron emerged from the doctor's office. When I enquired as to what was wrong, he replied that he had been severely reprimanded for not getting a repeat prescription for the medication he had taken home with him from the hospital. The result was that he now had to have a gastropy, which involved inserting a camera into the stomach to look at it. The consultant told him that because he had not kept up his medication, his ulcer had likely reappeared. He would have to take the medication for the rest of his life to prevent the ulcer recurring. When Arron spoke to a friend who had suffered an ulcer, he confirmed that he was taking the same medication as Arron had been taking, and would continue to do so for the rest of his life.

It was a very worried Arron that I eventually took to the hospital for the gastropy. When he emerged, however, his face was beaming. He told me they had found no recurrence of the ulcer and that he wouldn't have to take any medication. Arron had been my lodger for many years and had viewed my talking to unseen things with a great amount of fear and disbelief. From that day forward, he was a little more accepting of my abilities and told everyone I had healed him.

In order to be a certified practitioner qualified to use Bush Flower Essences, I needed to submit several case histories. I now had enough to earn my certificate based on the merits of my case histories. I now had several certificates -- two for the chromo therapy course I had taken; three for the Reiki one, two, and Masters; and one for the flower essences. Did that make me an expert? I remembered something else Dad had taught me: Never let anyone call you an expert. He believed that if you accepted the title, it opened you up for a fall when you made a mistake. (He told me an **ex** is a 'has been' and a **spurt** is a 'drip from a tap.') To this day, I never let anyone call me an expert, as I am constantly learning. I have learned as much from my children and students as I have from my Angels, and am always open to new ideas and understanding.

What had I learned?

(1) I needed to constantly heal myself in order to be a good and proficient healer of others.

(2) Dreams can deliver powerful assistance and advice if you are able to decipher them.

(3) Acceptance of everyone for who they are, not who you think they should be. Every interaction is an opportunity to learn. If another person's demeanour or behaviour annoys you, examine it. It probably mirrors something you don't like about yourself. Listen to your gut instinct. Be discerning, as there are no hard and fast guidelines. Learn to like yourself. Be honest with yourself and open to change.

I vividly remember waking up one morning with a teacher's words resounding in my head: "Give them milk and honey." I never cease to be amazed at the depth of understanding these words convey. You need a fertile bull and a cow to create the calf to facilitate the production of milk -- a holy trinity. Fertile, healthy males and females procreate to continue the rhythm of life. The honeybees' hierarchical system is made up of drones, workers, and the queen. Without the queen, the drones and the workers are redundant; without the workers and the drones, the queen is redundant. The hive with all its components is the perfect set-up for life on earth. Likewise, road sweepers, brain surgeons, the angry, and the timid are all vital components of life on earth, the University of the Soul.

(4) Flower essences are powerful tools to aid in healing and locating deeply hidden memories that have created a pattern of dis-ease in life from within.

(5) I had something called cellular memory, which began before I was born.

(6) I had found one male I could begin to trust -- Adam.

(7) Certificates do not bring clients to your door or put money in the bank.

What was the universe teaching me?

Expect the unexpected. Miracles can happen more than once in a lifetime. Your thoughts create your experiences. Dad wasn't always right in his thinking. His perception was shaped by the life he had led and the conditioned responses he had put in place to deal with all eventualities. He shared his old learning with the most precious thing in his life -- me. He loved me more than life itself, he often told me.

There were people in my life who helped me address my 'old' conditioning -- like Adam, who wasn't afraid to sing his own praises or broadcast them to the world. This didn't make him a 'big head,' as Dad had referred to such people; he was merely acknowledging his attributes. As we began to share our journeys of discovery, I soon realized Adam was good at acknowledging both positive and negative aspects of himself.

Shortly before his death, my father underwent an operation to correct a condition known as glaucoma, or 'tunnel vision.' I could now see how the way he thought and dealt with life situations had created a predisposition to developing this form of disease and I made a mental note to try and balance what he had taught and impressed upon me at all times.

CHAPTER 7

Birth Frequency Healing and the Three Musketeers

There is usually a good reason for everything that happens in your life. This includes the people and the situations in which you find yourself. Taking responsibility for your part in every relationship, circumstance, and situation is crucial to the healing process. Every time you hear yourself attributing blame to circumstance or another person, ask yourself, "What is my part in all of this? What part am I responsible for? What is the universe showing me?"

With this in mind, I went to see my friend Bill for my first birth frequency healing. He was pleased and excited about what he had learned in the birth frequency workshop he had attended. Over the ensuing weeks he had found a way to put a person's birth frequency through his cymatics machine, which was basically a computer that created specific frequencies of sound waves to achieve a given or expected result when applied to the human physical form.

At the workshop he had attended, he was told about a woman who was constantly having nervous breakdowns, despite being in a happy family situation with no obvious problems in her life or mental illness. The minute she was introduced to her birth frequency, she remembered being in the womb with her dead twin brother. At the time, she didn't know she was a twin. After asking her mother, she found that she was indeed a twin and hadn't been told in order to spare her pain. This little case history sparked my interest, after having discovered the seeds of my anger during my experience with the flower essence.

I was my usual sceptical self as I lay on the therapy couch preparing to experience what Bill had been raving about. The minute the machine was turned on, I felt lightness and a joy I rarely experienced in my life, especially since meeting and marrying my ex-husband. My mind was transported to a magical place that felt like home. The visions continued for about half an hour as I excitedly described my exhilaration to Bill.

Over the next couple of months, memories of childhood incidents, emotions, and feelings began to surface. From my perspective as a healer, I began to see how I had created the opportunities for learning that were now present in my life. Dad had always taught me to never be too 'cocksure,' as he put it. He told me I would never know everything there was to know and that I would always be able to learn. Although this was good advice, it appeared that I getting close to where I could manifest my teaching potential, based on the information I had amassed so far about the journey of the soul in the University of Life.

I had two more birth frequency healings over the course of nine months, each of which produced a different result. I came away from one seeing little rainbows floating everywhere. I came away from the other feeling responsible for something I had no idea what to do with. My intention was to introduce birth frequency as part of my system of healing, but I didn't know how to do this. As usual, I searched for the answer.

It was around this time that Doris the Reiki Master contacted me. She was selling some crystals and I went to have a look at them. I told her about the birth frequency healings and what was going on in my life. She had previously asked me to make her up a flower essence and during our conversation said that a flower essence from me was equivalent to a healing. That was praise indeed, I thought, considering the source.

I had also learned much more about making up flower essences. I had established that my electro magnetic field drew negative energy like dust to an ioniser. I knew that if I made up a flower essence without first preparing myself and cleansing my energy field, some of the frequencies I was carrying would end up in the flower essence, thus contaminating the pure vibrations of the flower.

It was from this conversation that Doris suggested I run some workshops from her healing room. I wasn't sure if I should venture into such uncharted territory, but with Doris' encouragement, I eventually put together two workshops -- one on flower essences and the other on positive focus.

I held the positive focus workshop first. Adam attended that one. I had established a format for the day, but as soon as I began the workshop, I took off in another direction. Two of the people attending the workshop were a mother and daughter whose husband and father I had tried to heal. I vividly remember Gordon and the acute pain and suffering etched on his face a he lay in bed with prostate cancer. Anne had recommended that he see me. His wife loved him dearly. They had a wonderful relationship and two smashing kids. It had been hard to watch this kind, gentle man suffer.

I went back to see Gordon several times. Miracles were being expected of me and I felt overwhelmed by the responsibility. I remembered when I had been healing at the hotel and had wanted each person to feel a change and know that healing had taken place. I wanted each one to go away with hope for the future. My thoughts at the time had turned to Jesus and how he had performed miracles. My first reaction to these thoughts was that I wasn't Jesus and never would be. Then Dad's common sense and logic came to the fore. At no time would I ever profess to be as profound, brave, and unconditional as Jesus. After all, I am human, I told myself. Then I listened to what I was saying to myself and remembered that Jesus was also human. If he could heal like that as a mortal, then surely I could aspire to that same level of excellence. Then and there, I affirmed that I wanted to heal to the highest level I could attain and make a difference in the lives of the people I touched. (I also affirmed that I didn't want to be crucified as Jesus had been.)

Gordon eventually died, but only after experiencing much suffering and radiotherapy treatments that caused both his upper arms to snap. Before he died, he underwent an operation to insert steel plates to repair the damage.

I felt I had failed. I was upset and miserable. Never before had my soul felt such a strong urge to give up.

Four years after the positive focus workshop that Gordon's wife and daughter attended (where his wife had made the positive focus affirmation that she wanted to paint and hold an exhibition of her paintings), I found myself buying the local paper again -- the same one I had bought when I was looking for my lost dogs. The first page of the paper fell open, revealing a woman I recognized. She had just held an exhibition of her paintings in Norwich. It was Gordon's wife. Because she had been such a timid little thing at the workshop, I hadn't held out much hope that she would find the courage and self-esteem to carry out her goal. A mini miracle had occurred where I hadn't I expected it.

Ever present in my mind was the memory of the powerful effects the birth frequency had on me. I truly believe that every disease has a specific frequency. According to the laws of physics, two 'like' frequencies cancel each other out. If this were true, I reasoned, then wouldn't it be possible to tune into the specific frequency of whatever disease I was treating and cancel it out? My gut instinct told me not to do it, and I listened. Common sense told me that if this were true, then every disease would have a specific frequency that I could also channel. I couldn't help but remember my first healing experience on the woman who later had a cataract operation. I had been in danger of manifesting that disease within myself.

What about the birth frequency? Surely I could channel it if Bill gave me the specifics. But again, common sense and gut instinct deterred me from channelling someone else's birth frequency in such a way. For the time being, I gave up. I obviously wasn't meant to use this method of healing, I told myself.

I was content to look after my horses and my two children and perform healings. I was still conducting the bi-weekly groups, but began to notice I wasn't as fit as I had been. I had been completely drained of energy after taking the Reiki course, but thankfully that had subsided. During the next few years, healing seemed to tire me. Also, when I went to Glastonbury with my friend, I found myself constantly out of breath trying to climb the hills near where we were staying. My friend got quite angry with me. She encouraged me to climb Glastonbury Tor.

"You just have to try," she curtly told me. "Walk through the pain you feel in your chest, and it'll be fine."

I tried, but the pain got so bad it would have taken all day for me to reach the top. I gave up and went back to my tent to sleep. I attributed the lack of energy and breathlessness to changes in my energy field as I increased the power of my healings. I had noticed right at the beginning that healings always left me with a dull pain in the centre of my chest. I had also experienced strange dizzy feelings when I first began healings, almost like being in front of your body instead of in it. I was quite happy to bear the pain and discomfort if it meant I would evolve into a better healer and teacher.

I phoned Jeremy, the spiritual teacher, and asked whether he thought I should see a doctor and if so, how I'd explain what I was doing and how it might be affecting me. He agreed it was probably a side effect of my development as a healer. All healing energy comes through the heart chakra. I was aware that expansion and use of this chakra can cause very real physical pain.

The girls we called the Three Musketeers had asked me if they could do Reiki one with me. Warren offered to let me use the orangery at his home to teach the workshop. The Three Musketeers had been coming to my groups for approximately two months. Having seen the positive results on her horse Warrior, Wallis was keen to begin. The first day passed with no incident. I was very pleased with the way the girls were learning to use their intuition; they were miles ahead of where I had been when I had first started out. I was able to show the girls an easy format they could use quickly and with great skill.

I had another tool in my healing chest that was helping me find my answers when stumbling in the dark. Most of what I was learning and teaching was based on actual experience, voices or thoughts in my head, common sense, and simplicity, along with a little science and physics. Several years before, while learning the tarot, I had come across a deck of cards with animal symbols. Each animal represented a spiritual lesson, opportunity, or confirmed what I was thinking at that specific time.

I can recall the first time I witnessed the phenomenon of animals arriving at important times in my life. I was talking to my friend Sandra on the telephone about something the thoughts in my head had been teaching me and doubting the validity of what had been said. As I spoke to her, I looked out my window into the garden and saw five little birds fly down from the top of the tree and look right at me. By then I had become accustomed to animals appearing to me visually in meditation and to my students, and I would rush eagerly to my book to see what it meant; however, I had never experienced animals appearing in the flesh like this and sitting in a tree looking straight at me. I excitedly told Sandra about the birds and also got my lodger, Arron, to look at them to see if he could identify the species. I decided they were baby blue tits that hadn't yet developed the black feathering on their heads. By the time I put the phone down, I had forgotten all about the birds.

It was several days later when I remembered them and went to my book to look up what a blue tit signified. The page dropped open at 'nuthatch.' Its message was 'the grounding of higher faith and wisdom.' That convinced me that the five birds were indeed nuthatches, a species I had never before seen in my garden and have never seen since. The picture of the nuthatch in Iain's bird book was identical to the birds in my tree.

I strolled around the grounds of Warren's estate, lost in thought, looking for guidance as to where my path was leading. Various birds called out or exhibited some odd behaviour, which signalled a message or a clue for me. I am happiest when I'm working with my horses or in nature. The animals and their language has become a way of life for me. If I am ever in doubt about something I was planning to use in healing or with the way I am dealing with a situation, help in the form of thoughts in my head always arrives first and then an animal verifies it for me. The animals help me to recognize the positive assistance I am being given and separate the fuzz and rubbish from the truth and the facts.

On the second day of the Reiki workshop with the Three Musketeers, Warren offered to take us for a walk around the grounds of the estate and show us the Heronry there. I thought it would be a wonderful place for us to do meditation. It wasn't difficult to find the heronry as it was breeding season and the noise was deafening. I thought about meditating somewhere else, but my guidance was firm and strong. We sat down and made ourselves comfortable. I could sense the girls' uneasiness with trying to meditate in such a noisy place. I led them into the meditation, announcing to my utter amazement that once we began, the herons would shut up. My goodness, I thought, I'm going to look like a proper idiot in front of these new students if that doesn't happen. To my astonishment, the noise stopped completely. Not even a cluck emerged from the herons. As I proceeded, I was told to say that a magpie would call out, signifying the correct use of occult knowledge and familiars. As predicted, the magpie called out at the appropriate time. I was then instructed to announce that a jay would call out, signifying the correct use of power. And so it went, with my announcing that a particular bird would sing or call out and the event happening as predicted. My confidence grew with each announcement and arrival. Towards the end of the meditation, I had the girls focus on their heart centres. I told them they would see an animal, and asked them to remember it when we had finished the meditation.

When we came out of the meditation, we opened our eyes and sat there looking at each other, wondering if what had just happened had been real or merely a figment of our imaginations. I had never before experienced such a powerful incident with any own animals, let alone wild ones. The Three Musketeers sat next to each other on a large log. I sensed three energies behind me.

"Okay," I said to the girls, "I have three energies behind me. Tune in as I have taught you and tell me what you get."

Bev gave me a colour, which I recognized as a signal for a particular energy. I encouraged her to name the energy, and to my amazement she gave me the name I associated with the arrival of that colour. I turned to the girl on the opposite end of the log, who gave me a colour and a name, both of which tied in with my own messaging system. I was very pleased with the rapid development and understanding of these girls. At last I had found my vocation!

Wallace, the third student, had the most difficulty understanding what I was trying to teach. When I turned to her, she announced, "Well, I got God." This caused me to stiffen. Jeremy, my spiritual teacher, had told me that I was here (on earth) to work for the 'big chief." I had interpreted this to mean that I was indirectly connected to Him through his minions, the voices in my head. Not for one moment did I think that He would consider me important enough that He would appear as an unseen energy behind me. I chose to believe that Wallace was mistaken in her interpretation, and said no more about it.

We walked back to the Orangery in a dazed silence, each one mulling over what had just happened and trying to make sense of it.

As we walked, Wallace suddenly said, "You didn't ask us what animal we got when we tuned in to our heart centres."

."Okay, tell me what you saw," I replied.

"I saw a Golden Eagle."

I gasped in amazement. The Golden Eagle is the Native American symbol for God.

This latest revelation in my understanding and development rather unsettled me. I had always believed in the existence of something we called God, but He had never seemed to answer my prayers. I didn't like dealing with a subject over which wars have been fought. Furthermore, it was difficult enough to get people to understand their own unacknowledged, unused, stagnant abilities without trying to bring God into the equation. I suddenly envisaged even more folded arms and crossed legs at my talks and workshops. I put that one on the back burner for the time being, and chose not to think too much about it.

Having God right behind me also reminded me of my first typist job. My supervisor, who didn't like me for some reason, would sit right behind me. She'd look over my shoulder and shout at me about a mistake I had made before I even had time to correct it. Every letter I threw into the rubbish bin was frowned upon and considered a waste of precious company paper.

After the incident at the Heronry, I was asked to do a healing on a lady named Trish who had irritable bowel syndrome. I began the healing in my usual way. I spoke to Trish at length about her childhood and probed for any incidents that might have caused her to be fearful and nervous or with which she would associate emotional pain. She recalled one incident of deep pain related to the death of a grandparent and another that I don't recall anymore. She also gave me her age at the times of these incidences.

As I proceeded with the healing, a voice came into my head, strong and clear. I was told to tune in to the parts of her brain that held her memories at the ages she had given me. I proceeded as instructed. After the healing, I asked Trish what she had experienced during the healing.

"It was strange," she said. "When you asked me about painful incidents in my life, I came up with the death of my grandparents. But while you were healing me, I suddenly recalled a vivid, long-forgotten memory. I was at school and my dad had given me too much dinner money and he wanted the change. I put it in my desk and was seen doing so by two girls sitting behind me. They were from a very religious family, so I trusted that they wouldn't tell anyone or steal the money. When the money disappeared, I knew they had taken it. My dad was very angry and went to the school. The school administrators refused to believe what I said, citing the girls were from devoutly religious families and would never do such a thing. They accused me of spending the money. I forgot this incident after a time, and it is only now that I realize how much it upset me. The other incident I remembered while you were healing me was not the pain of the death of my grandparent, but the fright of seeing a black figure on the stairs."

I gave Trish some exercises to remove these fears from her cellular patterning, and for two years she remained free of the disease for which I had treated her. She has not done anything to move forward with her life, however, and to this day tolerates a controlling, aggressive, manipulating husband she confesses to not loving. Consequently, her irritable bowel syndrome has returned.

After healing Trish, I had a call from her father, Bob. He had been diagnosed with lung cancer and the doctors wanted to operate on him. He was toying with the idea of coming to see me for a healing. He had been to a local spiritual church and believed somewhat in life after death. I told him I would program some healing sends into him. When I did the sends for Bob, I experienced the most powerful transition of energy I had ever encountered. I also had a notion to clear certain acupuncture meridians, something I had never encountered before. About a week later, I phoned Trish to find out how she was getting on and to explain that the healings I had sent her father might make his tummy upset. She laughed and said that was exactly what he had been experiencing. When Bob went back to the hospital, they found that his tumour had vanished.

Three years later, I received a call from Bob, who told me that the cancer had returned worse than it had been before. I told him he would need

Jeanne Ames

to come and see me and that we would look at emotional healing in order to effect a complete healing. Bob turned up for the healing in an extremely expensive, shiny new car.

"I will pay anything for a cure," he told me.

I assured him my normal fee would suffice and that part of the healing process was his responsibility, that part being to clear the emotional cause of his dis-ease. Bob was used to paying for what he wanted. If the doctors didn't seem to be moving quick enough or he had a long wait for an appointment, he went private and paid. He approached the healing with the same attitude, although I knew this was one situation that money could not fix. If we were to achieve any kind healing, I had to get him to acknowledge and begin clearing his emotional baggage. Try as I might, I couldn't get him to acknowledge his emotions, change his diet, or even stop smoking. At each session, I gently probed. It turned out that Bob had been badly let down by his mother. He told me he had forgiven her, but I didn't feel he was being honest about his true feelings he was somehow diminishing the way he felt or not acknowledging the depth of his emotional torment. Sometimes as human beings with rational intellect we know that we should forgive and we therefore do it verbally before we are really ready to let go. This creates dis-ease. It is far better to acknowledge that you do not quite have the amount of forgiveness to actually let it go or find balance and continue on working on that aspect than to convince yourself that it is all done and dusted and let it fester and grow under the surface becoming emotional baggage. If we could all snap our fingers and offer unconditional love to every one and everything never getting angry or afraid we would all be happy on the Earth in the University of the Soul. It is far better to acknowledge your less attractive traits, thoughts, desires and emotions and at least that way you can begin to balance and eradicate them. You cannot heal or clear a behaviour pattern that you do not acknowledge exists. No matter what I did or said, I just couldn't get him to deal with these issues and release them.

In desperation, I made a tape for Bob, which I hoped would reprogram his subconscious and help release the deep resentment he felt about what his mother had done. At the very least, I hoped to buy him some time so he could heal his hurt and resentment. I put together a positive focus programme for him, complete with little cards he could place in certain strategic spots to reinforce the positive programming from the tape. I also used background music with subliminal positive messages. Bob would phone me every Saturday morning and we would have long conversations about life in general and his exploits as a young man. Although he insisted my meditation tape helped, he eventually succumbed to the cancer. I was deeply saddened when I learned of his death. Once again, I felt somewhat responsible because I had failed to heal him. I had used every tool in my formidable arsenal of healing tools, and still he had died.

I spent the next couple of weeks mourning in solitude. Then a BFO struck me (a blinding flash of the obvious, as my Aussie friends called it). I could use what I had learned while healing Trish, i.e., I could use brain memory to recreate each individual's birth frequency. I didn't have to channel the frequency; I just had to tune in and send energy to the parts of the brain that held the memory, and the frequency would be recreated. If I had cellular memory and brain memory of my time in the womb, then I must also have my birth frequency memory. I began experimenting on my clients. I carried out my normal procedure for healing and added some birth frequency healing. Without exception, each client recalled far distant and long forgotten memories that had deeply disturbed him or her in childhood.

What I needed to do now was prove that I could teach this method of healing to my students. My new friend Sally had come onto the scene by now. Natalie and Adam were getting ready to move back to Australia when Sally arrived. She had done Reiki One with my original teacher and had experienced the same negative reaction as I had. She did Reiki Two with me. Some weeks later, Sally phoned me for help in sending healing to her friend's son who had tried to commit suicide. I tuned into his energy field and had a look, something I had learned to do since I had seen the demonstration of Jeremy unhooking the energy from me. I gave her a format to do a distance send of healing, which included a send of lemon to his area nine and ten.

"Don't worry," I told her. "It will probably give him diarrhoea, but he needs this to get rid of the 'shit' in his life."

A very excited Sally phoned me a week later to tell me that her friend's son was much improved and had indeed experienced an acute attack of diarrhoea. "I didn't think I could do that," she said.

I had already experienced the power of such sends while working with animals that were at death's door. While unfazed by her enthusiasm, I was pleased someone had finally realized they had the same abilities as I had and knew how to use them correctly.

I had been shocked when Nat and Adam told me they were going back to Australia, as we had become very close. I knew the Universe had decided we were becoming too insular, having been drawn to each other by wisdom; knowledge, and understanding that flowed freely whenever we were together.

I needed a place where I could do my healings. As usual, the Universe arranged it for me. My friend Warren and I were discussing his fruitless efforts to establish a healing centre at his Estate. When I left, I suggested we work on it meaning we should make an affirmation to try and find a solution whilst out of body at night. That weekend during an open day at the Estate, a lady approached Warren.

"You should have a healing centre here," she said.

Within three days, she had sent him a cheque for £3000.00 and the healing room was born.

What had I learned?

(1) I had experienced my birth frequency, which enabled me to bring to the surface and heal the deep emotions and memories from the womb and throughout my whole life

(2) Miracles don't always happen where and when you expect them to. Whatever you give will have a positive and valued effect somewhere, a situation I see repeated in my life to this very day.

(3) Gordon's wife wrote to me after his death to thank me for giving them hope. She said I had made the last weeks more bearable for them. I have had several visits from Gordon since his death. He is very happy where he is, and is proud of his wife and her achievements, which she would probably never have undertaken if he had lived.

(4) I learned to let go of my responsibility for other people's life or death. I understand that each individual is responsible for his or her own emotional dis-ease. No matter how powerful a healer I may be, I simply cannot cancel it out with my healing tools. Such a result would bypass the learning in the University of the Soul.

(5) God can come right up close when He or you choose.

(6) As a teacher, you should never be deterred by a student's apparent inability to grasp what you are saying. Each individual will find a way of using the knowledge you are bestowing upon him or her. I couldn't see how Wallis would become a healer, as she struggled so hard to understand the concepts. God chose her to convey this message to me.

(7) I found a way to implement birth frequency healing without having to put myself as risk.

(8) Birth frequency healing works in much the same way as a wound heals itself. When a child is conceived and the sperm meets the egg and develops into the first cell, at the centre of that cell and every cell created thereafter is a string of chemicals known a DNA. The chemical messages in this DNA are responsible for cellular renewal and repair of the body from birth to death. Humans are constantly in the process of cellular renewal and repair. When a wound occurs, chemical messages are read from the DNA that created the human form in the first place, and cells are created that repair the wound according to the DNA blueprint. The body will always return to a state of balance according to this blueprint. This chemical messaging system for renewal and repair can become contaminated and distorted by a myriad of emotions or what is eaten, drunk, or experienced in this life. By recreating the birth frequency, the body begins to remember its original blueprint without the contamination and attempts to return to its original balance. Birth frequency healing is just one way to stir what is deeply buried or not acknowledged. The lessons of the University of the Soul cannot be bypassed.

(9) I found a way to use birth frequency in healing and to pinpoint it accurately by utilizing a person's own memory.

What was the universe teaching me?

Never underestimate your students or the value of what you are sharing. I am not responsible for anyone except myself. Every question you create is a signal to the Universe to provide an answer for you to find.

CHAPTER 8

Proof of the Pudding and Australia

There is an old saying, "The proof of the pudding is in the eating." I now had a new tool to use in my healings when I thought appropriate: birth frequency healing. I knew from past experience that introducing this method of healing too soon could release such deep emotion that the client may never return. I was careful to use it wisely and only after I had established trust with that client. There is no point in drawing out the emotions until the person is ready and willing to look at them. If done prematurely, the client will file away these buried emotions in the same (or possibly another) 'filing cabinet' such as the liver, kidneys, an arm, a joint, or a leg, only have them resurface at a later date. It is impossible to bypass who you are and what you have created.

I needed to know that I could pass on the ability to carry out birth frequency healing. It had developed into a powerful healing tool for me, but I wasn't sure if would work for others. I decided to include it in 3a under the heading "Reiki,' which was starting to cause me some problems because of its many misconceptions. Most of the misconceptions about Reiki were related to inadequate teaching, lack of understanding, and contamination from unseen "on the side" frequencies. It seemed that Reiki Masters were becoming ten a penny. First, there was a one-week course for Reiki One, Two and Masters that included a lovely holiday abroad. Then a weekend course was offered. From my perspective, I saw disastrous consequences for anyone who chose to undertake such a journey so quickly.

I also had a problem with the way Reiki was taught using symbols and attunements. The symbols were very useful in helping to solidify my confidence in my abilities; however, I found myself forgetting to use them. The results of my healings and sends never varied whether I used the symbols or not. Perhaps the attunement process and the use of symbols was a way of getting people through the door. In any event, I never encountered one single person who had a positive thing to say about Reiki. Was the Universe trying to tell me something?

Darkness is only Light not Switched On

I had another problem with the Reiki teaching. Every Reiki Master I encountered taught me that you could get Reiki only from a Reiki Master who attuned you. The story of Reiki as I understand it is that a guy named Usui spent years studying and teaching Christianity. One day, one of his students asked him why he couldn't heal like Jesus. This question moved Usui to give up his teaching and travel. His travels took him to Tibet where he studied ancient records that were written in a language called Sanskrit, which he could read and understand. When he had completed his travels and returned, he still didn't have the answer to his student's question. He decided to go up a mountain and fast and meditate until he found an answer. After twenty-one days, gold symbols appeared over his head and he saw a way to invoke the healing energy. According to what I have been told, he stubbed his toe as he ran back down the mountain and was able to put his hands on it and heal it immediately. After fasting for twenty-one days, he would normally have a light meal so he wouldn't get sick; however, Usui amazed everyone by eating a full breakfast. He began to use the symbols to attune people to the healing energy, and Reiki was born. If you cannot get Reiki from anyone but a Reiki Master, how did Usui get it? Wasn't he just a human being who took the time to look?

There is no good or bad way to find your destination. Reiki helped me find mine. My blindfolds were slipping, and the darkened room I had once found myself in was becoming brighter. Because I had made the choice to take those attunements and embark on a voyage of discovery, I had begun to make the changes needed to make my life meaningful, bearable and enjoyable. I had also benefited from the teachings of my dad.

I wanted to teach my loyal student and friend Natalie what I had learned about birth frequency healing. I was anxious to see if it would work in the same way for her as it had for me. We had a day session and Nat used what I had taught her on one of my original students, Brenda, and my daughter Marie. Sure enough, the process worked for Nat exactly the same way it had for me. I passed it on to Sharon, my Australian friend, and it worked for her. She carried out a birth frequency healing on Nat's mum Teresa, and the results of that healing confirmed what I had suspected. It was a powerful tool that worked for others who had been carefully and correctly developed and taught. I passed it on to Sally, who I would eventually ask to use it on me after I had come out of hospital and been given very little hope by the doctors and nurses (a situation I covered briefly in the first chapter of this book.) Once again, I would find myself on the receiving end of something I had taught. It was a good opportunity for me to experience the value of what I was teaching and bring definition to my understanding of what was taking place with these new healing tools I had been given.

When a pharmaceutical company creates a new drug, they must perform many tests, including double blind trials. In a double blind trial, half the test subjects are given the actual drug and the other half is given a placebo. Based on this, I came to the conclusion that even modern science acknowledges the power of the mind. The placebo double blind trials demonstrate the power of the mind to create disease or eradicate it. I was not prepared to teach birth frequency healing until I had tested this further.

With this in mind, I asked Nat to use birth frequency to heal one of the most difficult aspects of my life, my daughter Marie. After the difficult childhood she had experienced, Marie had created certain patterns in her life. I found it extremely difficult to communicate with her or help her in any way. She would never open up or talk about anything she was worried about, even as an eleven-year-old. When I picked her up from school every day, she would be in floods of tears. Although I tried every approach I could think of to get her to open up, she would never tell me what was bothering her. A year later, when she moved to her new school, she told me she had been worried about leaving her friend Naomi, who was a year younger than her. It turned out her fears and worries were unfounded, she soon found a new friend at the new school. Her attitude to life in general didn't change when she went to college and eventually found a job as a hairdresser. Again, I witnessed her suppressed tears and total misery when she arrived home from work. The woman who ran the shop was bullying her. I urged her to find another job where she would be treated better. Still she chose to put up with the state of affairs at work. Everyone else around her was sad to see her so miserable.

Eventually I persuaded her to see Nat for a birth frequency healing, hoping that someone other than her mum would inspire her to move forward. To my dismay, after the birth frequency healing, her relationship with her boss got worse and she was given a month's notice.

In retrospect, I realize that Marie had never truly communicated and was always stuck and afraid to open up or move. Her job forced her to meet people and to communicate. She had little confidence as a hairdresser and eventually took two jobs, one as a shop assistant and the other packing books. Life was now even more miserable.

One day she was sitting having a coffee at a restaurant in Norwich when she overheard two women talking about their search for a new hairdresser for their salon. Desperate to improve her situation, she plucked up her courage and introduced herself as a hairdresser to the women. She secured herself an interview and eventually got the job. She hated colouring hair and the job entailed only cutting and blow-drying. She was there for about four years, during which time her life changed. I watched her gain confidence in her abilities and in her work.

Was it birth frequency healing that brought things to a head, or just the Universe giving her a push in the right direction? Unlike chemicals, there are no tests I can run for birth frequency healing; only time and case histories reveal the bigger picture. I know how much it helped me after being diagnosed with cardiomyopathy. I have also watched clients recover from endometriosis, lifelong asthma, and make life-altering changes following such healing.

The voices in my head have told me many times that I had been chosen to participate in an experiment to determine how quickly someone could be taken through the development process. By 'development' I mean changing the operating frequency, allowing finer frequencies to get through. On many occasion, I would find the going very tough. During these times, I'd fondly recall Dad's words: "You've just got to wipe the blood from your nose, get up, and have another go."

Often when I was trying to find an answer or a way to do something with regard to healing, one of my dogs would become ill. Terrified of a vet bill I couldn't afford, I would immediately start programming in various healings. This is how my animals also helped facilitate my learning and my acquisition of the knowledge I would require in the future. It is easier to get a quick result with an animal because they don't have the added dimension of intellect; they just accept what is. (I must add here that if the method I used to heal my animals didn't work or if I thought they were in unnecessary pain and suffering, I would immediately take them to the vet.)

I was approached by the voices to take on another experiment. This time I didn't bother to ask what it was.

"No!" I loudly affirmed. "I've worried enough about sick animals."

A few months earlier, Arron had brought me a pigeon whose wing had been shot off. I didn't hold out much hope for Ollie, as we called him. I spent half an hour with my hands on him, programmed in a few sends during the night, and put him out in a quiet shed where he could eat and drink. I anticipated he would be dead the next morning. When I got up the next day, Ollie was on my mind. With more than a little trepidation, I went to see if he was still alive. Not only was he alive, but he had also eaten. I bandaged up his wing and Ollie became part of the family.

This had awakened in me childhood memories of my Uncle Henry flying tipplers and tumblers and how I had always wanted to own some of these beautiful acrobatic pigeons. Iain and I ended up at the local cattle market to buy some pigeons. We eventually acquired our pigeons, which sparked the passion Iain had been searching for. He is now a championship show judge.

Every bird we acquired was shown the same love and devotion, as were all our horses and dogs. We quickly built up a flock of about sixty pigeons, the favourite of which was a pure white tippler, who would fly so high she'd become a speck before tumbling over and over and pulling out at the very last moment. She was spectacular to watch and a much-prized bird.

About six weeks later, Iain noticed his pigeons weren't well. Despite meticulous cleanliness on Iain's part, one by one they became ill. We took them to a vet, who said they had Newcastle's disease. They were quarantined and visited by the Ministry of Agriculture vet, who took blood tests and confirmed the presence of the disease. The vet made quite a mess of it, as she had never tested pigeons before. I asked her more about the disease and if the birds would possibly recover. She said she had never heard of them recovering.

I was distraught. By the time a week had passed, we had a bin bag full of dead pigeons. I decided to take the remaining pigeons indoors and attempt to feed them by hand and give them healing. The only place I could safely keep them was in my bedroom; otherwise, our dog Abby would have made short work of them. I used all my healing tools -- colour, flower essences, and programmed sends. Eight birds survived.

During this time of intense focus on the pigeons, I began to think about their environment. I had been up in the spire of the church where my mum cleaned, and found it to be knee deep in pigeon excrement. I remembered the vet commenting he didn't often come across Newcastle's Disease, which is apparently another name for Fowl Pest pigeons. I thought about Iain and how meticulously clean he kept his pigeons. I was reminded of one of our first purchases, a bird belonging to a breed known as Shakers. When the bird arrived, we quarantined it for two weeks before putting it with the rest of our pigeons. Within a week, it became ill and died. The breeder sent a replacement, free of charge. The same thing happened. This time when we rang the breeder, he asked us what we fed our pigeons. After we told him, he replied, "Oh, I feed mine chicken pellets because they have antibiotics in them, which keeps them from getting ill."

Suddenly, a piece of the puzzle fell into place. Because the shakers were dependent upon a constant supply of antibiotics, they had no immune system of their own working for them. The chickens at the supermarket were full of antibiotics. No wonder people's immune systems were failing and all kinds of new diseases were cropping up. By eating meat from regular chickens purchased at the supermarket, everyone is in effect consuming a dose of antibiotics, much the same as the shakers. At that moment, I resolved to buy organic foods whenever possible. In fact, I would often go without rather than eat fruits and vegetables from crops sprayed with chemicals or animals injected with hormones and fed antibiotics. At the time I was a vegetarian, so the meat aspect didn't bother me; fruit and vegetables that had been sprayed were a different matter. I see no quicker way to confuse our internal chemical messaging system than by ingesting these chemicals in our food.

Contrary to what the vet had predicted, eight of our pigeons lived. I cried out in agony over the loss of our much-loved pets. How could such suffering have occurred before my very eyes? When I think about it now, I can appreciate the valuable lesson I learned about healing and, most importantly, about the immune system and the chemical messaging system. No matter how scrupulously clean you are, if you aren't ingesting the correct fuel in the form of food, then eventually the immune system will break down and disease will occur in one form or another. In our constant search to save money and prolong the shelf life of food, we have resorted to using hormones and selective breeding. In so doing, we are opening ourselves up to illness. We are lowering our defences by fogging our chemical messaging system with massive chemical input our body cannot process. This contaminates the birth frequency programming of our DNA -- our blueprint for survival -- which sustains the correct and balanced running of that machine we call the human body.

I began to include a 'tune-up' of the immune system in all my healings. Once again, the Universe had placed in front of me a learning process which, although emotionally painful, had provided additional information that would improve my healing success rate. (Contrary to what the Ministry of Agriculture Vet had told me I managed to save eight of the sick pigeons who all lived to fly free again and produce young).

Jeanne Ames

It was around this time that I went to see my old friend, June, who had been on the first Reiki one course I attended. She told me she was going to have her Rottweiller mated. I found myself informing her I would like a bitch puppy from that union. I couldn't believe what I had said! I already had far too many dogs. Why on earth had I said such a thing?

Later, as I was hosing and cleaning the yard, I started to chastise myself about wanting another dog. I immediately heard a voice, loud and clear. "Abby wants to come back," it said. Okay, I thought, still feeling reticent. Anything for Abby. I told myself that the dog hadn't even been mated yet and June would probably forget what I had said if the dog did get pregnant and have pups.

Two months later, I was told to phone June. Thinking something was wrong, I rang her, only to find that the bitch had been mated and was pregnant.

"I haven't forgotten you ordered a bitch," she said.

Eventually the litter was born and there were only two bitches. June said the puppy's mother's breeder wanted one pick-of-litter bitch, as she had the bitch on breeding terms and the other she was keeping for herself. I hid my disappointment, thinking if one of the little bitches was Abby and it didn't come to me, it would probably die. Sure enough, two weeks later I had a call from June telling me that the little bitch was fading. Normally I would have been over there in an instant, offering to heal the pup if at all possible. On this occasion, however, I knew it was not appropriate for me to interfere. I knew Abby wouldn't want to stay if she couldn't be with me. I wrestled with my conscience, hearing the disappointment in June's voice. Then I reminded myself she had done the Reiki one with me and had enough knowledge to know what to do. I knew I had to leave this one alone.

Two weeks later I received another call from June. The little pup was still alive. A friend of hers had phoned just after she had put the phone down from our call and offered to take over some fading puppy mixture, and the pup had survived. When June told me the pup was mine, I heaved a sigh of relief. My dilemma was over, or so I thought. I decided to go and see the pups the following week. Unlike all previous occasions when she had pups, June refused to let me see them. I had an uneasy feeling that was confirmed later when June called to say I couldn't have a pup after all, as the breeder had decided she wanted a bitch after all. I was shattered.

As far as I knew, Abby was trapped in a physical body in a situation she had not expected. I explained the situation to June, who knew and respected my healing abilities and beliefs. She knew exactly how I'd react when I was told I couldn't have the puppy. I sat panic-stricken, wondering what I could do, short of stealing the pup. I heard a familiar voice. "Don't worry. You'll get Abby. She is the pick-of-litter bitch, not the little one."

Now, up until this time the voice in my head had told me some pretty amazing things that had come true, but this was really stretching the imagination. The mother dog's breeder showed her dogs and had many champions, as did June. I really couldn't see the pair of them letting me have the pick-of-litter bitch. I must admit I was tempted to work on it. Deep down, I knew that this would be gross interference with the natural flow of things, so I refrained. If the puppy was meant for me, I would know which one she was and she would come to me.

Two weeks later June called to tell me that the breeder was coming the following day to choose her dog. If she took a male, I could have a bitch. I was still a little worried that I wouldn't get the right one. That night I resolved to go out and work on getting the right dog. I also made the affirmation to get Nat to help me. I told Natalie nothing about my affirmation. Early the next morning she called to say she had experienced a weird dream in which Abby came back. I laughed and told her why I was laughing.

"You might have told me what you were up to," she said.

Half an hour later, June called to tell me the puppy was mine.

The day came for me to pick up Isa. When Nat and I arrived, June met us at the door with a guilty look on her face. "This is your pup," she said. "I'm keeping the little one, as I've grown fond of her after all the healing I did on her."

I laughed. "It was the pick-of-litter I wanted," I said, and left. She looked mystified.

If I was a little unsure that I had Abby back, Isa (as I named the new puppy) dispelled all doubt within days. At eight weeks, she immediately attempted to open the round-handled doors just as Abby had done after I had changed them. Isa was eight and a half weeks of age and had had no prior experience with door handles, having been reared in an outdoor kennel. She like Abby soon mastered the round door handles. When Abby was alive, I always went to a particular pet shop and came home with treats for the dogs. I would keep the treats on top of a cupboard in the house. After picking up the shop's scent on me, Abby would immediately go the place where I kept them and ask for one without hesitation. I had owned Isa only a few days and there had been no treats on the top of the cupboard since I had brought her home. After returning with treats from the pet shop, Isa went to the place where I kept them. She sat and looked first at me, then at the shelf, just as Abby had done. That was enough to make me believe Abby had returned in the form of a Rottweiller.

I suddenly developed the notion to write a book. This took me on a search for a word processor. I went shopping for a word processor and came home with a computer I knew absolutely nothing about. Iain set it up for me. Before he left, he told me to make sure I shut it down before switching it off. I turned it on and looked at the screen, not having a clue what to do next. Frustrated at my own stupidity at having bought something I had no idea how to use, I tried to find a way to shut it down. I just couldn't get rid of the picture that filled the screen and shut it down as Iain had showed me. I phoned Nat, who told me to click on the little 'x' in the top right hand corner and then go down to the start menu on the bottom left. I had sat for almost an hour trying to figure the darn thing out, and all I had to do was click the 'x.' I had no chance with this, I thought.

Slowly, with Nat's gentle encouragement, I learned how to use the computer. The printer I bought came with a £200 voucher off the price of a holiday. I had an insurance policy that was due to pay out soon, and came up with the idea of meeting Sharon halfway between the UK and Australia. Adam suggested Bali, then added that since I was going that far, I might as well go all the way to Australia. Sharon agreed to meet me in Bali. Considering my previous fear of going to London, I must say I rather surprised myself at my eagerness to take this trip. I trusted Sharon completely; she knew my fear of travelling and had met me in London and guided me without fail.

I booked the trip and invited the Three Musketeers to join me in Bali. Two agreed, but the third couldn't afford it. After everything was all booked, Sharon pulled out at the last minute, so the two musketeers and I travelled to Bali. Then I would travel on my own to Australia, where I knew Sharon would be waiting. It was no different than travelling from Norwich to London, I told myself. If I could do that, I could travel from Bali to Australia. Again, one of Dad's sayings popped into my head: "In for a penny; in for a pound".

What had I learned?
(1) I was not happy with the title of Reiki, the heading under which I operated using my healing therapies.

(2) Birth frequency healing was something I could teach to others who were experienced enough to use it wisely.

(3) For me, Isa was absolute proof that dogs do return from past lives to live again.

(4) Thanks to a bunch of pigeons, I learned that what we eat influences what we create. I learned the painful lesson that no matter how powerful your healing tools are, sometimes you have to just let go and know you've done enough, without feeling responsible or guilty.

(5) I could travel to Australia, trusting that Sharon would meet me at my destination. Somehow I would find my way if I just trusted the instincts I was born with.

What was the universe teaching me?

To overcome the fears I had allowed to overwhelm me after my strongest protector and the person devoted to me had died (my Dad). I was given a format for birth frequency healing, which I was using wisely, having observed the way Reiki was being used in some instances. I had witnessed and experienced the havoc unseen energies could wreak when used improperly.

CHAPTER 9

Communicating with Masters and Angels

My first experience with the Masters of Wisdom was when the voices in my head started calling themselves 'The Masters of Wisdom.' I am suddenly struck by how schizophrenic I must sound when I refer to them as "the voices in my head," but this is the only way I can describe how I get the information that has helped me change my life and write this book. The voices in my head do not speak out loud; they arrive as thoughts. The only way I can describe it is this: If you had an argument with someone and are still seething when you leave him or her, you would probably mull the situation over in your head. When the voices in my head speak to me, the conversation is similar to the type of dialogue you might have with yourself if you were trying to figure out a plan of action or analyze something going on in your life.

After communicating with these unseen voices for five years, I was as confident and trusting of their existence and help as I was of any doctor. Much of the information I was given while performing healings or trying to understand a situation turned out to be correct. Invariably, though, I wouldn't understand it at the time.

Only with the benefit of hindsight would I eventually understand the meaning of the message I had been given or written down. Some months later, I would be looking for something and would come across a channelling. I would realize instantly that I had already been given guidance on events that had occurred in my life. This not only reinforced my communication skills but also gave me reassurance that I wasn't schizophrenic and wouldn't be taken away by men in white coats!

After I acknowledged that I was merely a normal human being with my sixth sense switched on, it struck me how hazardous and difficult my journey had been. If this book serves only to makes readers aware that they, too, have a 'sixth sense' and it's okay to use it, my purpose in writing the book will have been realized.

Throughout my journey to create a safe system of healing, my affirmation was always to provide all types of people – including those who scoffed at the thought of Masters of Wisdom or life after death – with healing tools so they could open up to their own journey of discovery. If they use these tools to create peace and harmony within themselves, then, like ripples on a pond, those feelings will touch every living thing around them, either by the spoken word or just by the natural flow of one electro magnetic field to another. My goal was to teach the world to sing!

In response to this affirmation (teach the world to sing), the universe began preparing me for travel. I had booked the tickets to Bali for myself and the two musketeers, thinking I would have Sharon to accompany me on the journey from Bali to Australia. Since I had committed to the trip and paid for the tickets, I was not about to back out.

About a year before my trip, I began getting very specific visual confirmation of the presence of the Masters of Wisdom. It all began one evening when Arron and I were sitting in my living room watching TV. Suddenly the room began to fill up with a milky haze. It was strangely still. Arron, who had become a little more comfortable with what I did after I healed his ulcer, began shifting uncomfortably in his chair.

"I don't know what's going on," I said. "This room is full of energy." I closed my eyes to try and determine what it was.

"What is it? I haven't done anything wrong, have I?" he cried out in sheer panic

"No," I reassured him.

For the next twenty minutes, circles of multi-coloured lights moved around the room. When they had gone, all I could remember was the name Dolores Cannon and the name of a musical group.

The next day, I told my friend Sandra about the experience. Later that morning, she arrived on my doorstep carrying a book called 'They Walked with Jesus' by Dolores Cannon. In the book, a woman who used hypnosis to treat her clients had come across a few people who had past lives connected to Jesus. I recalled my first affirmation about the level of healing to which I wanted to aspire.

Based on my school and bible studies, I believed Jesus was someone who could put his hands on a blind man and make him see. I also knew that if the emotional cause of the disease were not healed, then complete healing would not take place. As I read the book, I gained a clearer understanding of my healing practice. I am careful when using the name of Jesus, just as

I am careful when using the name of God; I never put myself in the shoes of either one of them. I am just plain Jeannie Ames, who is trying to get a handle on this thing called life.

I spoke to my friend Lucy about my experience, and told her the name of the group (Depeche Mode).

"I have only one album by that group and it's called Songs of Faith and Devotion," she replied.

Coming on the heels of the book by Dolores Cannon, I now trusted that the voices in my head would move me forward. By this time I had changed the name of what I was doing to 'Crystal Clear Diamond Healing.' I had woken up with the name one morning and immediately seen its significance. "Crystal' because I use crystals; 'Clear' because I was aware of 'on the side' influences; and 'Diamond' because a diamond's perfection reflects and refracts all the colours of the spectrum. When the name came to me, I recalled a vision I had had while having my final birth frequency healing with Bill. In this vision, I was sitting in a truck used to transport coal down a coalmine. I knew instantly it was the name for what I was doing. I understood that diamonds came from coal. Perfect.

I left England with the two musketeers, fully prepared to holiday in Bali and then work in Australia. We arrived in Bali at midnight. Men with guns stood over my suitcase and ordered me to open it. They had honed in on the bottles of flower essences I had brought along. They didn't speak English very well. I crumpled at the thought of having to explain that the bottles contained only brandy and water, not drugs. I looked at one of the men -- a big, fat, aggressive-looking individual -- and said, "Flower essences." Immediately, he waved his hands around and babbled to a colleague. Then, with an attitude that seemed to imply that I was 'one of those weirdoes," he waved me through customs. Not a good start, I thought.

As we headed to our hotel, I noticed the streets were lined with ramshackle huts. When we proceeded through the gates of the hotel grounds, I was extremely aware of the opulence compared to the streets and huts surrounding them. We settled down for our first night's sleep, all in the same room.

In the morning, we awoke to the pleasant surprise that our stay also included free breakfast. (I had been told we would have to pay for all our meals.) We rushed through our breakfast so we could change and begin working on our tans. Since landing in Bali, I had felt unsafe, which I attributed to being in a foreign country and the fact that Dad was not around to bale me out if anything went wrong. I looked to my usual place for comfort, the Masters of Wisdom, and got nothing. For the first time in a very long while, I felt completely alone.

That evening we decided to leave the safety of the hotel grounds. Another guest had informed us that the hotel food was extremely expensive and pointed us in the direction of a restaurant further down the beach. We arrived at the restaurant and found a table overlooking the beach. After we ordered our food, Wallis pointed to an object on the roof and said it looked like a rat. Sure enough, a huge rat was walking across the roof in our direction. As we ate, it scurried down the post right beside us. This should have been enough to send us scurrying back to the confines of the expensive hotel; but it wasn't. After several expeditions to find a cheaper place to eat, Catherine became ill with something known as Bali Belly. Now, anyone suffering from diarrhoea knows that it's awful enough without three of you sharing the same room. The inevitable happened and I, too, became ill. Wallis sat in the single bed with her legs drawn up in the foetal position. She had not yet succumbed to Bali Belly. Despite how ill I felt, I had to laugh

The next day, in an effort to get away from the stench in our room, I wandered down to the pool and met the woman who had sent us outside the hotel in search of cheaper food. It turned out that her husband had also been ill with Bali Belly. She proceeded to tell me that the only way to get rid of it was to take antibiotics. She told me to go outside the hotel grounds and barter with a taxi driver to take you to a Chemist who will know what to give you. Then I was to barter with the Chemist about the price for the medicine. Exhausted by my foray to the pool, I went back to the room and told the two musketeers what the woman had told me.

The two musketeers went out and after much haggling got the antibiotics. We slowly began to recover. From that day forward, we ate only the expensive hotel food. Then we began to notice something. A feeling would come over each one of us, followed by intense nausea, and then I would receive a communication from the Masters of Wisdom. After this happened a couple of times, when the old familiar nauseous feeling overcame us Wallis would look up at me and say, "They're here, aren't they?" Sure enough a communication would ensue, thus I began to recognise a familiar bodily feeling at the approach of these communicating energies which was recognised by the two friends accompanying me on my holiday, although the communication was always with me the presence was without fail felt by the others.

Jeanne Ames

My conversations were always silent two-ways, with my asking or responding with my thoughts and then receiving an answer. The only way Wallis and Catherine could tell I was conversing was by the nauseous feeling the Angels' presence invoked. Invariably, it happened at mealtimes.

"I don't know if I have Bali Belly or if they are here," Wallis would announce.

The holiday wasn't enjoyable for many reasons; not the least of which was the illness. I also found the abject poverty of the people outside the hotel difficult to bear. When the people begged, I witnessed tourists bartering with them to pay the smallest amount possible, say 20 pence for a baseball cap when the equivalent back home would cost up to £20. These people were scratching out a meagre living. A pound would not have gone amiss from the tourists' pockets. Yet, there was this need to get everything for a ridiculously cheap price.

I didn't experience the visual presence of the Masters of Wisdom until the final day at the hotel. The rainbow of lights circled the bathroom as I took a clearing bath to ready myself for my seven-hour flight to Australia.

I left the two musketeers at the hotel. They were itching for the holiday to be over so they could get home. Upon my arrival at Bali airport, I checked in and found a couple of English ex-patriots on their way back to Australia. I made sure to keep them in my sight at all times to avoid making any mistakes Sharon was waiting for me at the airport. As we talked that evening, I began to relax and feel safe for the first time since leaving England fifteen days earlier.

When I awoke in Sharon's flat the next day, I breathed a huge sigh of relief. I had done it! I had travelled on my own and arrived at my destination on the other side of the world.

Sharon wanted me to teach Reiki one to her mum. After explaining the change of name and my reasons for it, we set out for her mum's house in the Blue Mountains. I still felt weakened by the illness I had suffered. We stopped at a café for coffee and toast. I couldn't eat the whole slice of toast because my stomach was still so unsettled. We took the train to the Blue Mountains. I was relieved to discover that her parents' house was across the road from the train station, as I still experienced pain in my chest, arms, and legs if I walked too long a distance. I put this down to the fact that I was there to work and to the effect the energies had on me when they were close.

Over the course of the weekend at Sharon's parents' house, I was asked to do a couple of readings. I attuned Sharon's mum to what I now called CCDH. Sharon's father was very interested in what I was doing. He had ventured into different areas of healing himself and had cured his own bone cancer. We had a very enjoyable weekend.

Sharon started her new job on the first Monday of my stay with her, a job she had been waiting for all her life. There I was, alone in my friend's flat on the other side of the world, far away from everything familiar. Come on, Jeannie, I told myself. Go out and have a look around. It really was a strange feeling being so far away from home and everything that was safe and secure. I missed my animals and the familiarity of England. When I wandered out to the shops to buy food, I felt as though everybody knew I was from England without even talking to me. I felt painfully shy and conspicuous. Each day as my confidence grew, I ventured further out, eventually ending up on Bondi Beach where I would spend the day resting and sunbathing.

The following weekend, I stayed with Teresa, Nat's mum, who I had met during her visit to the UK. She had done Reiki one with me, which had led to my journeying to London and being met by Sharon. During my visit, she decided she wanted to do Level two. It was a spur of moment decision; she had been saving for it and decided she wanted it then and there. I hadn't brought the material I normally used to teach it, but I gave her the workshop and promised to send her the literature. We had a wonderful weekend. Teresa's Dad Rene drove us to a beautiful restaurant on Sunday. On Monday, Teresa took me to Manley, when I saw Sydney Harbour for the first time.

As Teresa and I sat in the boat in Sydney Harbour enjoying the sun, the voices began again.

"You can go home in two weeks. You will have done everything you came here to do," I was told.

I had purchased an open-ended ticket. "Good," I replied, feeling a little homesick. At that moment, I felt Teresa, who was seated beside me, tugging on my arm. When I looked at her, she was pointing skywards.

"They're here," she said.

"I know," I replied.

"I can see them," she said. "Look! Look!"

I looked at where she was pointing, but saw nothing, although I knew they were there because they had been speaking to me.

When I had arrived in Australia, I was told I would find a certain crystal. So far, all visits to crystal shops had been extremely disappointing. I had seen nothing that I would even remotely be tempted to purchase. The first shop we entered after leaving the boat in Manley had tarot cards, crystals, and crystal healing bowls. I was immediately drawn to a rather dark corner where I found a medium-sized crystal labelled as amethyst. I held it up to the light and saw the ridge of gold running right through the centre. I knew it was ametrine. I had been looking for a good piece of ametrine. Ametrine is the name given to a crystal that is made of amethyst with citrine, another form of crystal, running through it. It was also of a formation known as elestial, a very powerful and unique combination. I had read that ametrine reprogrammed DNA and I was anxious to work with it. I had not been able to find a suitable piece in the UK and yet here I was on the other side of the world and I had found it wrongly labelled in a dark and dusty corner of a shop. I bought the crystal and was told the energies would meet us again in the middle of the harbour. I was to hold the crystal in my hands and a frequency would be passed through the crystal to me. I told Teresa about my communication and she couldn't wait for the return journey.

We sat contentedly eating fish and chips overlooking the beach at Manley, happy to be experiencing the wonderful thrill we were feeling in each other's company and with our shared experience. To date, no other living person had ever experienced my visits from the voices as Teresa had. No one had seen them arrive or leave in the way she had. It was such a relief to be sharing the experience in such a way for the very first time. It would not be the last time I would share such experiences with friends.

We got on the boat well ahead of schedule for the journey back to Sydney Harbour, and settled ourselves on the top deck right at the front of the boat so we could get a good view of the harbour. I removed the crystal from the brown paper wrapping in preparation for what we would experience in the middle of the harbour. Teresa looked at the crystal and I gave it to her to hold.

I had experienced the attunements of Adam and Nat and Teresa, where each one seemed to have left their body for an uncomfortable length of time, so I was accustomed to their energies and their long departures out of body, which was just as well because little did I know it that Teresa was about to exhibit the same phenomena right there on the boat! I handed the crystal to Teresa and the next thing I knew, she was gone. Her body was sitting bolt upright and rigid. Her eyes were closed and she was unresponsive to my voice. Mild panic overcame me. Here I was, on top of the Sydney Harbour Ferry with a bunch of people I didn't' know and my friend Teresa, who was sitting with her eyes tightly shut facing skyward, clasping the crystal in both hands as if her life depended on it.

I tried to call Teresa back, but there was no response. As we neared the middle of the harbour where I had been told to have the crystal in my hands, I wrenched it from her grasp and sat with it in my hands as inconspicuously as I could. Again, Teresa began tugging my arm, gesticulating skywards.

"They're here! They're here!" she said.

"I know," I replied, trying to stay calm.

She gave me a blow-by-blow description of what was happening to the colours in the sky. First, they moved above me. Then a light travelled down to the top of my head. I gave up trying to avoid attracting attention. Instead, I closed my eyes and enjoyed the sensations and feelings that were coursing up and down my spine.

When we arrived back in the harbour, we were a little unsteady on our feet and held each other's arms for support. I gulped a few swigs of my bottled water in an attempt to ground myself so I could walk on legs that felt like cotton wool.

"I'm taking you to Nat's favourite bookshop," Teresa declared. "It's quite a walk."

The walk was uphill. I found it difficult and was breathless, but so was Teresa. It's just the energies, I told myself. Drink more water and you'll be grounded.

We walked from the harbour to the bookshop known as the Adyar, stopping every so often to draw breath and gulp down some water. The Adyar is a huge bookshop in Sydney, supplying books on esoteric subjects, crystals, and various other associated items. Teresa took my bag and suggested I look around. The first book that caught my eye was an Alice A. Bailey book entitled 'Initiations Human and Solar. Wow! An Australian guy had previously told me in a reading that I was up for another initiation. I had suspected that when a developing soul masters certain aspects of his or her sixth sense and life in general, an initiation would take place. This book seemed to confirm my theory. I had never heard anyone speak of such a thing until he had mentioned it, and now here was a book on the subject written by an author I greatly respected. I had to have it, so it went in my basket.

As I continued to browse through the books on the shelves, I was amazed to discover books about different Masters of Wisdom. If these guys were so well recognized that books had been written about them since the late eighteenth century, why had no one else in the English healing fraternity heard of them or even acknowledged their existence? I left the Adyar laden with books to read during my days alone in Sharon's flat.

Except for a few visits from people who wanted readings, my time was my own during the following week. My recent purchases now forgotten, I went through Sharon's collection of books and came across one that contained a Clown Exercise that involved drawing and colouring a clown. What you draw, how you draw it, and what colour you choose apparently reveal your hidden self.

I got a piece of paper and drew the clown. I was very confident that my inner self would be revealed as confident and balanced. What a shock I got when I looked up the various aspects of what I had drawn. True, I was totally balanced and grounded spiritually, but I apparently had no grip on life! This analysis helped me to recognize that after finding two people to become CCDH Masters, I had actually been packing my bags to go; in other words, I had been preparing to die. I had always found life on this planet difficult. I had thought all the old programming had disappeared, but there it was, staring me in the face. I thought about it long and hard. I had plenty of time away from family and animals. Would I be happy to go now? Could I trust my people to take CCDH forward and teach the world to sing? What if they didn't and I was 'over there?' All my trials and tribulations, learning, and understanding would be wasted.

I decided I needed to make some affirmations about staying. I quickly wrote two affirmations, both of which I cannot remember. The third one was 'I am absolute.' When I looked at the words I had written, they didn't make any sense. 'Absolute' was not the word I wanted to use, but try as I might, I couldn't find another word to take its place. I folded up the piece of paper and put it in my bag, making the resolution to go out and work on staying alive that night.

Two days later, I pulled out the Alice. A. Bailey book I had bought. It fell open at a page that read 'seventh initiation absoluteness.' I rushed to my handbag to see if that was indeed what I had written on the paper when making my life affirming affirmations. It was.

My next weekend trip was to the Blue Mountains to visit Adam's Mum and Dad, who had bought their hundred-acre farm on the strength of a spiritual teacher they had met. When I spoke to Adam's Dad Neil about the old Tibetan who often appeared during my meditations, he said it was probably the Master DK that Alice A. Bailey had talked about. Until this revelation, it had never occurred to me that such a learned energy would seek to work with me. Because of their content, the Alice A. Bailey books had earned my greatest respect from the moment I had started reading them. What Neil said made sense. I began opening up to the possibility of knowing the identity of the Masters of Wisdom. Adam's parents had a number of books on the subject.

I spent my days at the farm reading or walking. Neil and Margaret decided to do CCDH. Neil had already done one in the UK, so I took him through two. Margaret was an experienced healer, so I did the same for her. During the workshop, the Masters' communication was much stronger and clearer than it had been in the UK. I received communication from new energies I had never heard from before.

I also did some research on the acupuncture meridians. One of Teresa's friends, an acupuncturist, wanted to meet me. I extended my stay for a week so I could meet him.

I travelled back to Sydney by train. Teresa met me and escorted me back to the bus stop so I could find my way back to Sharon's flat. I had several days to digest what had transpired. I wasn't entirely happy with the information I had managed to piece together so far, so I made an affirmation to work in a certain way at night. I didn't like having to continually deal with 'on the side' interference. It was a nuisance and I wanted to decrease or eradicate it. I was determined that no person I taught would suffer the ignominies I had suffered. If possible, I would find a way to define who and what I was working with in a way I could easily relay to others.

I returned to the UK brimming with confidence about taking CCDH forward. I did some channelling with Nat and the Masters of Wisdom, but I still didn't feel I was heading in the right direction. I continued working at night in the way I had affirmed in Australia, but my health took a real dive. I had absolutely no energy, which I put down to changing frequencies and possibly jet lag. No healings were arriving for me to do and my bi-weekly groups were dwindling. Just as well, I told myself. After all, I had no energy, fell asleep at the drop of a hat, and felt quite ill.

About four months later, Paul, a man from whom I had previously had a reading, emailed to say he was coming to the UK. I had met him through Nat and Adam and had travelled to see him for a reading with my friend Sandra. I thought my students would enjoy receiving guidance from someone other than me. We arranged for Paul to come and stay with Nat and Adam and do a few readings for some of my students. Paul had been channelling the Masters of Wisdom for about eighteen years and is the author of a book called 'From Atoms to Angels.'

My horse Hyvoy had been accidentally let out with my stallion the previous year. By the time I returned from Australia, it was evident that she was in foal. A gift from heaven, I thought, trying to convince myself that I could cope with an addition to our already large family of animals.

I booked myself in for a reading with Paul. When I arrived for the reading, I had an excited phone call from Iain to say that Hyvoy had just given birth to a filly foal. I had spent sleepless nights during the last two weeks out in the stables waiting for the birth, yet I had still managed to miss it!

"What are you going to call her?" Paul asked.

"I don't know. Any suggestions?" I asked.

"Well," he said, "you could call her Violet Flame."

"No," I replied. "That's much too prissy."

Paul commenced the reading. Well!" he exclaimed. "I normally channel the Masters of Wisdom. I've done so for fifteen years and know them like the back of my hand. However, I have two energies here that I do not recognize. Do you know who they are?"

I had worked with two energies since I had begun to get names, and had not passed on this information or even acknowledged their existence as my teachers to anyone. I recognized these two energies and had learned to trust them over the years. In fact, I trusted them as I had trusted my parents.

"Well, if you think you've seen energy, you ain't seen nothing yet!" Paul said.

Wow! I hadn't told anyone about my night time affirmations regarding the way I wanted to work. In a very short period of time, I had attracted exactly what I had been looking for. The energies Paul was describing were exactly what I had asked for.

The next morning I awoke with a name for my filly foal on my lips -- Seraphim Violet Flame. When I told Paul what I was going to call her, he screwed up his face in puzzled recognition. I had heard of Sandolphin along with the Masters of Wisdom, but I had never come across the name Seraphim. I asked Paul if he had ever heard of the name before. He said it was strangely familiar but didn't recognize it. Serry, as we now call her, is a beautiful chestnut and will be four this April 2003.

I decided I had used my married name for long enough. Every time I signed a cheque or credit card slip and saw the name, it created an immediate feeling of deep discomfort within me. On the same weekend as my reading with Paul, I had a numerenergy reading with his wife. We examined the numerology of my birth name and my married name and I told her how uncomfortable I was with my married surname. I decided to change back to my maiden name legally, in the UK it is done by a process known as deed poll and add 'ne' to Jean because it felt comfortable and I liked the energy. That's how I became Jeanne Irene Ames. Boy, did it feel good!

What had I learned?
(1) The Masters of Wisdom, with whom I had worked for the last five years, were occasionally visible as moving circles of multicoloured light.
(2) I was definitely not schizophrenic.
(3) To travel.
(4) I learned that what I felt on the surface was not what was in my underlying programming and cellular patterning. I didn't know myself as well as I thought.
(5) The Masters of Wisdom are known by many. Their existence is acknowledged and written about in many books.
(6) You can choose who you want to work with. If you are not happy and comfortable and feel a need to change, the way will be shown.

What was the universe teaching me?

To build confidence in myself and what I know. To believe in my gut instinct. This doesn't mean I'm too cocky; it just means I know what I know. To live in a bigger world than the universe I had created for myself when Dad had died.

CHAPTER 10

Angels and Esoteric Acupuncture

I was very excited about the information Paul relayed to me during my reading. Based on what Paul told me, I knew my affirmation had created the desired results After all, he knew nothing of how or with whom I worked. We had never done a workshop together; in fact, I knew him only from my two readings with him.

With Paul's help, from what he confirmed in my reading, I knew I had learned a simple method that enabled me to identify and communicate with whatever energies were teaching me. This unique language was shared with no one except my trusted "guys." I was taught very simple, easy-to-learn techniques to ensure I was not being misled or misguided. I later taught these same techniques to others so they, too, could create their own form of recognition and language with their angels.

I had finally received the clarity I needed regarding my Angels. For me, it was imperative to receive physical, verbal proof of their communication. Every day in this journey of discovery I stepped out into unmapped territory and worked with unseen voices and energies. I needed this kind of evidence to help me follow the signposts my life laid out for me.

Believe it or not, I view myself as a very down-to-earth skeptic. The information I had discovered regarding the Masters of Wisdom had helped alleviate my concerns about what I was doing. I often found myself in what I term "pinch me" situations, where I would wonder if I was really experiencing things or just imagining them. Of course I had heard about Angels, but for some reason had never envisaged them choosing to work with the likes of me. When Jeremy, the spiritual teacher, had told me there was an Angel holding a sword at my side, I took it with 'a grain of salt.' At my first reading with Paul some years earlier, he told me that the Michael I was continually hearing in my head was, in fact, Archangel Michael trying to get through to me. I had resisted this notion, however, and had instead interpreted it as a signal for me to visit Jeremy.

I received some valuable advice from Jeremy. During one of his weekly group meetings, he said that holding on to a spirit guide could keep you at one level and you would not evolve or develop. From then on, I avoided tuning into any one specific energy. One day I was driving in my van after completing a healing some twenty miles away. I became aware of four angels in the van with me. I waited for a communication and none came. I didn't feel uncomfortable. My life was full of accompanying energies; I knew they were probably there for a reason.

That evening, I told my friend Bill, who had carried out my birth frequency healings, about the Angels in the van. At the time, I hadn't bothered to look for names, but as soon as he asked who they were, their names tripped off my tongue.

"Oh," he said. "They are the Angels of the four directions."

I might have asked more, but I was leading a group. By the end of the session, I had forgotten about it.

Several days after the second reading with Paul, when my foal Seraphim was born, I was drawn to a particular book related to tarot that I had bought some six or seven years earlier. I usually buy books on impulse. After looking at a page or the introduction, I usually know right away if a book is for me. When I arrived home with this particular book, however, I found I just couldn't get into it. I put it on the shelf and forgot about it. (Unfortunately, I no longer have it and have no idea what it was called.)

As I scanned my bookshelf for inspiration, I absentmindedly picked up this book. It fell open at a page that listed a group of 70 plus Angels known as the Seraphim. Wow! Now I knew what these new energies were -- a hierarchy of Angels known as the Seraphim. There they were, all numbered and named. Back when I had first begun to hear the voices in my head and found confirmation in Australia that their existence was known to others, I had no idea there were groups of Angels. If I had read this book then, I most certainly would have considered my communication with them to be a figment of my imagination. I had been extremely lethargic after my return from Australia. Since I could no longer attribute this lethargy to jet lag, I assumed it was as a result of the new angels and their intense energy.

It took about two years for me to 'change channels' and open up a clear dialogue with these new Angels. I had become accustomed to the way in which the Masters of Wisdom communicated. Thanks to Jeremy, I also had built-in safety devices to check the validity of who and what I was talking to, not the least of which was my strong gut instinct. The guarded approach to strangers and the outside world that I had learned from my parents also served me well in my spiritual encounters.

Around this time, I began having long conversations about healing with a local delivery man, which resulted in his mother requesting a healing on their dog Molly. His mother Jessie harboured a lot of emotional pain. I find that animals act as processors for the energy the owner is carrying in his or her electro magnet field. When I visited Molly (who happened to be Abby's granddaughter), she was lying in her bed, looking thoroughly fed up with life. She had lumps on her lymph nodes and had been diagnosed with lymphoma. She had been given about three weeks to live. I began the healing and started talking to Jessie about her life, after which I made up a flower essence for Molly that would protect her energy field. I visited Jessie several times over the next few weeks. She was terrified at the thought of losing Molly, the only living thing she felt she could trust. Jessie told me she was also seeing a vet who was an acupuncturist and a healer. Having met this vet at a healing fair and seen her case histories, I sent her mine in the hopes we might be able to work together. I desperately wanted to work with animals; I found working with people to be quite challenging.

In a previous chapter I wrote about my old Doberman Khan, who had been diagnosed with lymphatic cancer. Molly also had a biopsy that confirmed it. On about the second or third healing I performed on her, I was told to tune into certain acupuncture meridian pathways. (You may recall that I had done the same thing when I sent the healing to Bob, and it had produced a good result.).

That afternoon, Jessie phoned me excitedly. She had taken Molly to the acupuncturist vet for her twice-weekly acupuncture session and upon examination, no lumps could be found. When the vet placed the needles in the usual points, they immediately fell out. When Jessie asked her why, she said this typically occurred in animals when there was no need to clear those particular meridians.(I hadn't told Jesse that I had tuned into the acupuncture meridians and cleared them; I had merely carried out my Angels' instructions).

This was the confirmation I needed to begin adding 'Esoteric Acupuncture' to my healing tools. I would need to test it further, but I knew I had been given a valuable new tool to effect complete and permanent healing within a physical body structure.

I wanted more specific information about the acupuncture meridians. As I mentioned earlier, I had stayed in Australia to meet Teresa's acupuncturist friend, and we had kept in communication by email. One day he emailed me a website that was selling a CD-Rom with all the acupuncture meridians for horses, including a list of diseases and the precise acupuncture meridians that required clearing connected to any given specific disease processes. I bought the CD-Rom and waited for the Universe to send me clients. None arrived. A woman in the area was healing animals using a few crystals and a hammer, and she was loaded with clients. My business had dried up again. I longed to find a way to move forward and live in peace without being constantly drained, debilitated, and forlorn.

Around this time, I received another phone call from Jeremy. One of his clients, a healer who had been on TV, was struggling with a difficult client named Morag, who owned horses. I phoned the healer who had been dealing with Morag and he told me what Jeremy had said about her past lives and suggested she be persuaded to get rid of all her horses. He wanted to know if I would be willing to take her on as a client. At last, an opportunity to show what I could do and get people through the door for CCDH!

During our telephone conversation the healer tried to impress upon me what Jeremy had said about her past lives and the fact should not have horses. Now, I have had horses for thirty-five years, through two marriages, childbirth, and all the traumas. I consider them part of my family and have given them the loyalty, love, and respect my parents gave me. What the healer had said about the woman having to get rid of her horses struck a deep chord within me. When he handed over this client he suggested I just tell her she should not have horses. My response was that she obviously needs healing and counselling, and if she is not meant to have horses, she would see it for herself and make her own decision.

When I phoned Morag, she proceeded to confirm what the healer had told me. She had sixteen or seventeen horses buried on her land. After taking them in and seeing their pain from back problems associated with incorrect treatment and riding, she had had them shot to avoid passing them on to someone else. She told me that people even brought their sick horses to her and left them tied to her gate.

Morag lived in Scotland and was not about to pay me to visit her. After my experience with Bob and the distance healing, I had decided that my time was valuable and I should begin charging for it.

I explained the electro magnet field to Morag and how I believed it affected an animal's health. I cited the case of a woman named Shelly and her Old English sheepdog, Ollie.

Jeanne Ames

Shelly had telephoned just before I went to Greece with Sharon for a week's holiday. Iain had taken the call. (I had taught Iain how to tune in to people.)

"I'm sorry, but Jeanne isn't here," he said to the caller. "Can I help?" He was shielding me as I was very tired. Then I heard him say, "Okay, that's your dog. Now tell me what's wrong with you."

The woman had liver cancer and her dog had been diagnosed with liver failure. Iain took the number and I suggested that he take Shelley and the dog on as a case history to build his knowledge and understanding. He agreed, and before I left for Greece, I gave him a short format to follow. I returned from Greece to a jubilant Iain. Contrary to what the vets had predicted, the dog had lived and his liver was working fine. Shelly, however, was another story, and she called to book me for a healing. I visited Shelly and performed the healing in the usual way. Strapped around her waist was a bag that delivered the chemotherapy drugs to her over a forty-eight-hour period. Like Jessie, her life was full of deep hurt and pain.

Despite my careful probing, Shelly refused to look at any of the hurt and pain she carried. I saw her put all her emotions in an emotional closet. She was determined not to dig deep and release the pain and deep anger and resentment she held about her father, the eighty-three-year-old man with bone cancer whom I visited. When I left, I knew Shelley wouldn't call me back. I thought Iain might have a better chance. He was doing healings for free and was willing to travel thirty miles to do them so he could build his case histories and his knowledge.

He came home from one such healing and said, "I'm not going back again, Mum. I travelled all that way and tuned in through the crystal, just as you taught me. Then the phone rang. She got up to answer it and stayed on the phone throughout the entire healing. She didn't even bother to come off it to say goodbye when I left."

I couldn't help but feel that Shelly might have been a little more attentive if she were really interested in staying alive and had paid hard-earned cash for the healing. We left it to her to contact us, and didn't hear anything more until about a year later.

When Nat and Adam were staying with me, a woman knocked at my door. It was Shelly, but I didn't recognize her, as she had undergone chemotherapy and treatment for liver cancer. She informed me that Ollie, her dog, was ill at the vets again and wondered if I could do something for him. I looked at his energy and saw that he had had enough of his life and Shelly's tormented life, which she refused to acknowledge. I said I would do a send, but didn't hold out much hope. I took her out for a walk with the horses and, once again, laid it out for her as I saw it. She was pitifully unhappy about her life at the time.

"Make the changes required to move towards a happier life," I told her, "and you never know . . . It might not be too late. Ollie might stay."

"No, I can't," she insisted. "I just don't want to go there."

I did the send to Ollie and heard later that he had died around the same time. Shelly died a few months later. As far as I know, there was no apparent reason for Ollie's death. Shelly, however, died as a result of the liver cancer.

Six months after her lumps disappeared, Molly took to her bed and refused to get out, eat, or drink. They had her put to sleep. It broke my heart.

Jessie, Molly's owner, refused to look at her life and make the changes required to bring her peace. I needed to distance myself from these healing relationships, so I severed all communication.

Several years later, I bumped into Jessie at the local pet store.

"I've got Molly back," she announced, as she relayed a strange story about a hooting owl and a chocolate Labrador puppy.

I have to admit I doubted her.

About a year later, I was driving down a country lane not far from my home when I saw a woman walking, or rather being hauled by, a chocolate Labrador. I looked at the Lab and instantly recognized my old friend Molly. As I quickly dismissed the silly notion, I looked at the woman. It was Jessie.

I explained to Morag how I thought it all worked and gave her the case histories I had to support my theories. We agreed that I would put together a healing programme for her, much the same as I had for Bob, and would begin sending healing to several of her horses free of charge. Morag paid for the time I spent working on her and I just wanted to help the horses any way I could.

Morag improved and so did the horses. I acquired a couple of case histories for my distance sending theories on colour and acupuncture. From my experience with Ollie and Molly, I knew that unless the animal's owner was able to release some of his or her hurt and pain, it was going to be extremely difficult to bring about complete healing in the animal. It also concerned me that Morag would not hesitate to shoot a horse if it was in any sort of pain.

Jeanne Ames

I soon began to receive daily phone calls. It became clear to me why the previous healer had been pleased to pass it over. A dressage horse had a problem with lameness. On top of that, one of his muscles, which had been incorrectly developed by improper training and riding, was now giving him big problems. When I tuned in, I also detected a problem with the blood supply in the veins in one of his hooves. There appeared to be a blood clot. Since an operation was out of the question, I went to my chromo therapy course notes where I discovered that lemon would dissolve blood clots. I put in a send and programmed it in several times a day for a week. A week later, the Farrier cut the horse's hoof back and was surprised to find blood flowing in the sole of his foot. I was not surprised. The frequency of lemon had done its work.

One of the other horses was just not right, although I couldn't pinpoint the exact problem. Morag became more terrified that another horse would have to be shot, so she ended up on the phone to me. I tuned in, did a send, and programmed in further sends over the following week. This time I detected several blockages in the acupuncture meridians and did the send to clear them. The horse spent most of the week lying down, but at the end of the week, he got up with no illness or discomfort.

Morag decided she wanted to do CCDH, including the element for esoteric acupuncture. I arranged to travel to Scotland to teach her, as she could not leave her children, husband, and horses. I was happy to undertake the journey, as I was eager for people to see, feel, and understand what they were capable of doing with CCDH. I spent three weeks with Morag and learned more about horses, their backs, and dressage than I had learned during the entire thirty years I had owned horses.

One more case history connected to Morag is well worth mentioning. Doris, the Reiki Master, had telephoned me again to inform me about another of her crystal sales. When I arrived, she showed me a crystal bowl. Aware of her skills as a sales woman, I vowed to leave without it and then return if I wanted it. I told Morag about the crystal bowl and my reluctance to part with my cash.

After we had hung up the phone, she called me back and said, "You have to buy that crystal bowl!"

"I know," I replied. "I've just phoned and am on my way to pick it up."

Several days later, I had a call from Morag.

"One of my sheep is down. She can't even lift her head. We had to put her lamb down. She must have missed her copper injection and the lamb had a problem with its nervous system. I've seen them like this before. I accidentally gave her a long-term acting antibiotic when I should have given her a short-term one. Even without the mistake, her chances aren't good. Having made the mistake, though, I thought it was worth giving you a ring. I don't think there's much you can do, but would you please just give it a try?"

I knew there was no time to waste. Sending healings sometimes takes awhile. This sheep was in imminent danger of dieing. I looked at the crystal bowl and reasoned that sound travels differently from light. It had a denser energy, so perhaps it would be a good idea to tie the healing frequency I was sending to the sound wave of the healing bowl. Couldn't hurt, I thought.

The shepherd looking after Morag's sheep arrived the next day, shovel in hand, asking where she wanted it buried.

"No need," she replied. "It's doing fine and suckling the lamb from the ewe that had three and couldn't cope."

I suggested that Morag talk to the mother sheep we now called Daisy to explain why her lamb had been destroyed and that she was getting a new one. I told Morag that if she felt a little silly talking to a sheep, she should just imagine what she wanted to say and it would be conveyed.

This reminded me of the conversation I previously had with a flock of sheep and with the plant during the chromo therapy course. I had never mentioned these conversations to anyone, as I was afraid people might think I was crazy!

Daisy ended up fostering two lambs.

What had I learned?

(1) The Masters of Wisdom were not the only energies from which I was able to seek help and guidance.

(2) Despite my efforts, I wasn't able to glean as much information about Angels from books as I could about the Masters of Wisdom. Yes, there were books, but I found them difficult to read. Consequently, I discarded what I had learned from my book research and started listening to my gut and the Angels.

(3) The more I listened to my gut instinct and my intuition, the clearer and more confident I became during conversations with others about what I was being told about my life, current events, or about another person's life during a healing or life path reading. The counselling module in the chromo therapy course had stood me in good stead. I was becoming conversant with the voices in my head, and was able to convert what was being communi-

cated into an easily understood format that I could relay to others. I became adept at two-way conversations, both silent and spoken.

(4) My body often reacted to these new energies. I would sometimes feel very sick after a communication. It was commonplace for me to throw up while eating a snack or during dinner and then be able to eat the rest of the food without feeling sick at all.

(5) Animals often mirror their owners' dis-eases.

(6) I could tune in and clear acupuncture meridians, both in person and long-distance, which appeared to target other vital layers of clearing problems in the disease process. I have been told and it is my belief that pre-disease conditions can be spotted in the aura before the disease manifests in the physical body. There are many levels of a disease process that need to clear before complete healing can be achieved. My affirmation was to heal a person as wholly as I could -- physically, mentally, and emotionally -- in an effort to ensure a disease did not return. The acupuncture meridians operate similarly to the wiring in a car or in the back of a TV; failure to treat a problem in the meridians usually results in the eventual breakdown of the entire machine. The physical body is no different. With the knowledge I had gained, I could now teach people how to cleanse their energy fields, tune up acupuncture meridians, and apply colour safely, quickly, and simply.

(7) I learned more about horses and the problems they suffer due to people's ignorance regarding balanced riding.

What was the universe teaching me?

When I was in Australia, I found myself in the middle of an emotional triangle of hurt, betrayal, and pain, the likes of which I had never experienced before. As I sat on the beach one morning pondering why I was here on earth, the enormity of everything I knew suddenly hit me. I had always been aware of people's emotional pain but had somehow managed to dull what I had felt over the years. My situation in Australia caused me to look at this more deeply. I sat alone on Bondi Beach, agonizing over what I had witnessed in each person in the triangle. I asked God how I could help. Despite having a basic understanding of how and why things were the way they were, I knew I couldn't heal everything. The reply came loud and clear: *Heal the abusers.*

"What about the animals?" I asked

"A way will be shown to you," I was told.

I had learned to speak to God without fear, knowing that I was worthy of his voice and his help.

CHAPTER 11

The manifestation of my affirmations after the Clown Exercise

By now I had become conversant with the Angels, having developed a system of communication similar to the one I had developed with the Masters of Wisdom.

I decided that my breathing difficulties could partially be attributed to a lack of fitness. Since my energy level had improved, Sally and I decided to join a local gym. My son Iain had decided to become a fireman, leaving me with all his pigeons to look after in addition to all my own animals. With my lack of fitness, I found the going pretty tough. I was also surprised to discover that I feared a visit from my ex-husband while Iain was away. I had never acknowledged this fear before.

I was certain that with all I had learned since coming back from Australia, things would begin to flow in my life on the healing/teaching front, but instead I found I was struggling with my health and with my direction. Where would I start, and with what? I had amassed a great deal of information through my experiences and I had no idea how to package it into a format that would be both acceptable and understandable to my clients.

One day Sally phoned and asked if I would like to go to the gym. I immediately agreed. I had been looking for inspiration; a swim and time in the sauna would be the perfect solution. Just before Sally arrived, Iain and I had coffee together. He said he wanted to start a business that he could operate on his four days off from the Fire Service. He said he'd been thinking of opening a horse feed business. I told him about one such business that had opened in our area; it had a delivery service that I had used on occasion. I watched the owner put every effort into the business, only to end up bankrupt.

"Yes," Iain said. "I remember that guy. What ever happened to him?"

"I don't know," I replied.

After our swim, Sally and I sat on the sideline and watched the people coming and going. A good-looking guy walked in.

"Now, if that guy were to chat me up, I'd definitely go for it," I remarked to Sally.

Without further ado, he walked around the pool, headed straight over to where we were sitting, and struck up a conversation with me. Out of the corner of my eye, I could see enough of Sally to see she was convulsed in a fit of the giggles. I struggled to regain my composure. Now that I was over Roger, I was open to meeting someone else; however, I was no longer experienced in flirting or being chatted up. I was so uncomfortable I fled to the sanctity of the sauna.

Opposite me in the sauna sat a large, kindly-looking woman, who appeared to be around my age. She remarked on my tan and asked where I had gotten it. During the course of our conversation, I discovered that her son was the man who had opened the horse feed shop and delivery service. I asked her more about it. From what she told me, I concluded that it was a difficult business in which to make a profit. Wow! I seemed to be manifesting quickly with my thoughts and what I was putting out there, I told myself.

Sally and I went to the restaurant for lunch. I was secretly hoping to get another chance to talk to the hunky guy from the pool. During our conversation, I mentioned that I felt directionless and was looking for a way forward. I told her that I wouldn't mind going to see Rosamund, the medium. The only problem was that there was a five- or six-month waiting list to get a reading, and I didn't want to wait that long.

Not long after I arrived home, Iain came through the door, grinning from ear to ear.

"I don't know if I did the right thing," he said, "but I was passing Rosamund's house and wanted a reading. When I knocked on the door, she answered. I asked her if I could have an appointment quickly for you and me. She said she hadn't known why but she had left two spaces open in her book, obviously for you and me. My appointment is next week and yours is the week after."

You shouldn't be surprised at this turn of events, Jeannie, I told myself. After all, this is what you teach.

I was so excited about the reading; it couldn't come fast enough for me. I remembered Rosamund saying to me at an earlier reading that I was the kind of person she would like to teach everything she knew. When I had relayed this to my friend Tracey, she had remarked, "Well, why doesn't she?" Good question, I thought, remembering Rosamund's comment that opening up to these energies was like putting your finger into a live electricity socket.

The information I gleaned during the reading about where I was heading confirmed what I already knew. In my energy field and occasionally around me, I could still feel the strong unmistakable presence of energy attached to my ex-husband. I didn't like this one little bit. I felt very unsafe when I felt its presence, and asked the Angels and the Masters of Wisdom to help release it. With assistance from the Seraphim Angels, I began to gather more information about clearing my energies and my lines of contact.

While talking to Rosamund, the card that showed up in most of my readings was once again on the table. She had previously told me that I had a psychic vampire. We discussed this dark energy. When she asked me what I had done to try and dissolve the link, I told her.

"Who have you been using to help you?" she asked.

"I usually go to Kuthumi (a Master of Wisdom) for help because I trust him," I replied.

"He's not really good for that sort of thing," she said. "Try El Morya. (El Morya is another of the Masters of Wisdom). A word of warning," she said. "If you decide to break the link completely, it could mean one of you has to die."

I didn't want to live with the link so firmly imbedded that I couldn't do my work in peace and safety. There was no way I could continue with it still in place. That night, I put up the affirmation to El Morya and began working on severing the links.

As I have mentioned, part of Rosamund's readings involved a hand reading. The line she had pointed to when she told me I had a psychic vampire was still present, although somewhat less prominent.

"Oh," she had exclaimed. "There was a point here where your chi had begun to close down. You were getting ready to go. And right here," she said, pointing to where the line became thicker, "is where you decided to stay. You must have been quite ill when this was taking place."

Still am, I thought. I finally had an explanation as to why my healings and teaching had dried up and why I had received no inspiration regarding a way forward. I was too ill to complete the journey safely. I realized I still had some work to do.

In an effort to determine what needed to heal within myself, I began taking some of the Himalayan Flower Essences. I had used them quite a few times and found them to be helpful in locating and clearing old memories that were causing me to react to certain situations in my life and undermine my health. The day before I prepared an essence, I would always establish my clear intention and ensure that I emptied my mind of all thoughts. Then I would go up to my room and be told what to put in the essence to help me release any difficult memories and heal myself. In an effort to become fit, I also used all my CCDH tools on myself.

After a couple of months, my enthusiasm to get out and bring CCDH to the world returned. One of my students, a woman named Jane, who taught psychology and whom I found very difficult to teach, had decided she wanted to become a Master in CCDH. She was one of those people who wanted what I had without having to develop it or take the time to learn and understand it. Jane taught me everything I needed to learn about patience. She was the total opposite of Wallis, the musketeer who got God in her meditation. I had learned from that experience that I was here to teach everyone, whether or not they would ever get the hang of what I was trying to impart.

Being a teacher of psychology, Jane thought she knew everything about herself. From my perspective, she had merely discovered something about her emotional undercurrents that needed balancing and, in an attempt to eradicate it, had adopted another behaviour equally as controlling and damaging. Patience is a virtue, I told myself. I learned much from Jane. The more I communicated with her, the more I learned about myself and the art of educated communication and counselling. I became confident that I could impart knowledge in a manner that could be easily understood and accepted by everyone – including those who might be tempted to challenge me.

It was around this time that two of the three musketeers, Wallis and Catherine, decided to hold a psychic fair at Warren's estate. This coincided with my inspiration to have an 'open day,' where I would invite people to drop in. This opened up events, which led to the local newspaper wanting to do an article on me. I readily agreed and a meeting was arranged at Warren's home. The photographer came and took a beautiful picture of me holding a crystal beside an Irish wolfhound I had healed. The interview was reported and published on a bank holiday. The female reporter did a fantastic job, and I couldn't have been more pleased with the result. This is it, I told myself. This is what Rosamund was talking about. You're on your way; no more hold-ups. Still, I felt more than a little daunted by the enormity of my task.

The newspaper article inspired me to arrange and publicize a talk about CCDH in the centre of Norwich. Quite a few people turned up. Sally and I had prepared a formal array of photographed case histories and written testimonials that people could browse through. Of course, the usual challenger showed up and created a scene. I admit I still had a rather full-on aggressive reaction to him, despite my attempts to eradicate this. Iain confessed afterwards that he thought I would actually punch the heckler. As it turned out, I dealt with him quite civilly and eventually he was silent.

From that talk, I picked up a few more clients for healing and met a couple more 'horse' people. One lady named Hilary read Thomas' case history with great interest and introduced herself to me at the end of the talk. She later telephoned to tell me about her Irish wolfhound that had been injured in a car crash and whose back legs were partially paralyzed. Later on in the week, she phoned to make an appointment. A couple of days later she phoned again to say she had to cancel the appointment. She had lost her job and couldn't afford to pay me. I was moved by her loyalty and love of her animal.

"Don't worry. Just come and I will do it for nothing," I said.

Hilary arrived with her dog. As I did the healing, I spoke to her at length. It turned out that the dog was also being treated by a therapist and a vet who did acupuncture. She was also taking him for swimming sessions. She told me she had difficulty fitting in the visit to me when I had wanted to do it, requiring an appointment much earlier than I normally started because of my having to tend to the horses. In order to save her fuel money, I had agreed to see her early, which meant I had to get up at five in the morning to get the horses done first. We continued meeting this way every week for about two months. Although there was little change in the dog's condition; I was committed and would continue treating her dog as long as she wanted.

Just before Christmas, I received a telephone call from Hilary. She informed me that a store near her was sold out of a particular doll she wanted and she would need to go to the Bury St. Edmunds store to pick it up. Since I lived on that side of Norwich, she presumed it would be closer for me, and asked if I would go get the doll for her. I declined, explaining that Bury St. Edmunds was a good hour's drive away and, just like her, I had to watch my fuel expenditures. She insisted that Bury St. Edmunds was nearer to me than her and intimated that I was being unreasonable. I came off the phone more than a little disgruntled. I had every right to say no, I told myself. Just what did she expect of me? I had never complained about getting up so early and getting to the healing room on time for her. I had made it as easy for her as possible. How could she treat me in such a way?

Jeanne Ames

The following Friday I arrived at the appointed time, but Hilary didn't show up. I didn't bother to contact her. I was saddened that I couldn't continue helping the dog, and tried to look for my lesson in this little saga.

I had quite a few people sign up for my new weekly groups. I was conducting one about animal healing and one about human healing. While I was running these groups, my little black mongrel Lolly suddenly became very ill. One morning, she started to act very strange and had a bout of diarrhea on the carpet before being sick. Within two hours, she was passing pure bright red blood and vomiting up the same. I laid my hands on her and programmed in some colours, but within an hour I could see nothing was improving and immediately took her to the vet.

I love all my animals, but Lolly was the light of my life. Perpetually willful but amusing, she was my constant companion. Losing her would have been like losing my right arm. After examining her, the vet didn't think her chances were very good, and he expected her to lose the entire lining of her stomach that night. She would have to be admitted and put on a drip, he said. Up until the time I held her on that table, Lolly had done her best to be her usual perky self. While she lay on the table, I felt her body go limp. The lights were on, but it seemed Lolly had left home.

I arrived home distraught, and turned immediately to my crystal. I had some knowledge of parvovirus, which was what the vet thought she had. I had done sends to a puppy with the disease and, contrary to the vet's prognosis, it had lived for a week. Because I didn't know the disease process, however, I didn't allow for or treat the necrotic material inside the puppy, her womb, or any of her organs. If I had known about the disease process, I could have put in a colour to adjust it.

Later, I got an opportunity to test my theory. We had a goat named Ambrose, who became ill while I was in Australia. The vet had saved his life, but said there would probably be a problem with the lining of his gut. His recovery would depend upon how much of it had atrophied. I immediately knew what to do and sent the appropriate colour directly to his gut.

It was while healing the puppy the CCDH way that I saw the value of using this method to introduce colour. I needed to use the colour indigo to curtail the hemorrhaging, but I was also acutely aware that the little thing was close to giving up. Had I introduced the colour through my chromo therapy lamp at that time, it may have died sooner. Indigo is similar to a general anaesthetic in that it reduces blood flow, numbs pain, etc. As it was, I was able to send the colour directly to the part of the puppy's organs I wanted to treat. In other words, I targeted the chemical frequency of indigo to the exact spot it was required.

I had a chance to use what I had learned on the goat. Within two days after I had programmed in the correct colour to re-establish a healthy gut, he was fine. Now Lolly needed my help. When I phoned the next morning, it was a very surprised young vet who told me she was still alive, although he still didn't hold out much hope. I continued to send healing to Lolly all that day. When I phoned on the third day, he told me he knew she was ready to come home because she had growled at him when he looked at her.

I arrived to pick Lolly up. She was right back to her old self -- on guard and barking at every moving thing. Having my best friend back made all the years of study and experimentation worthwhile. Funnily enough, the only one who was surprised by my triumph was me.

I continued working sporadically as healings came up and finished the evening groups. The groups were well attended. Everybody was pleased with what they had learned, including a certain mother and daughter, Hailey and Julie. I found out that Hailey had been trying to have a baby for years, but had had been unable to conceive due to her polycystic ovaries. Having completed the group meetings, she phoned to book an appointment for a healing. Over the next two months, I gave her a couple of temporary attunements to CCDH.

A temporary attunement lasts for thirty days. I had in the past sent some of my students to one of the new Reiki Masters in the area who was offering cheap attunements. I wanted them to spread their wings and hear other people's views, not just mine. You get put on a pedestal with all this stuff, and while you are on it, the people who put you there seem to spend most of their time trying to knock you off. I had fallen into the trap of allowing this to happen. I thought it was important for my students to expand their horizons and experience other forms of healing and viewpoints.

During one of their forays, a couple of them experienced a temporary attunement, although the Master attuning them told them it was permanent. After thirty days, both reported they could no longer feel the energy going through the palms of their hands in the same way. When I later became a Reiki Master and was given the formula for the attunements and knew how many it took for a temporary one, I could see why they experienced what they did.

At one of Hailey's healings, I was about to give her the customary temporary attunement, along with a formula she could follow to program in certain chemical frequencies she would need to ovulate, when I was told to give her only the formula she needed to ovulate. I did as I was told. An excited Hailey reported back the next time that she was now having regular periods. She continued her self-treatment without any attunements, and her periods continued. Before the healings and self-treatment, her periods had been practically non-existent. I have since received the good news that, after adopting two children, Hailey became pregnant in 2004, thus fulfilling a prophecy from one of her readings with me some years before.

What had I learned?

(1) Despite my inability to find helpful books about Angels, I began to build a strong impression of them. They were a great help to me when my dog was ill. They also assisted me with the healing and balancing I was trying to carry out on myself.

(2) The affirmation that I had made in Australia after completing the Clown Exercise (I wanted to live and take CCDH to the world) spurred a plan to which my body responded in conjunction with events in my life. This gave me the time, opportunity, and space to find what I needed.

(3) Action follows every thought. As I progressed in my learning and development, the speed at which this was happening was at times alarming to me. 'Beware of what you ask for' is a saying that comes to mind.

(4) Hilary taught me that I know what I know that I know.

(5) I was glad that I took up the challenge of my healing journey all those years ago and sought to gain knowledge every step of the way. My little friend Lolly is still here with me, thanks in no small part to the vet and that knowledge.

(6) People did not need the attunement process they could work with the colours and exercises I gave them equally well without this process.

What was the universe teaching me?

To take time for myself on the journey. Every thought and every action has a consequence.

CHAPTER 12

A return trip to Australia and flying with a new group of Angels!

After all the excitement of the newspaper article and my talk in Norwich, the public's interest in my work gradually died down. Once again, I was left searching for a direction. Through Iain, I had acquired a new friend named Donna, who was seeking help to find her way through a difficult situation in her life. Donna is an excellent nail technician. After I had complimented her on her beautifully manicured nails, she suggested I come to her salon to have my nails done. People always look at a healer's hands. With all the years of hard work and looking after my horses, my hands were a sorry sight. The system of nail care that Donna used was the answer to my prayers.

Her son Nathan was also interested in horses. They both did CCDH One with me just before Christmas 2000. Nathan was an excellent dressage rider, but had been persuaded by his father to give it up in favour of a college degree. Horses and dressage had been a huge part of his life. Upon meeting him, it was obvious he wasn't happy.

Around this same time, Iain had met a young woman named Annette, who became his girlfriend. Annette had endometriosis. Despite all my efforts to get him to send her to Sally for healing, Annette eventually telephoned me and booked a reading and a healing. I hated getting involved with Iain's relationships; I wasn't yet able to switch off what I had learned from Jeremy about distance scanning. I was dreadfully uncomfortable healing someone who was in a relationship with my beloved son. In any healing situation, I needed to remain non-judgmental and impartial. This was definitely a learning experience for me in more ways than one.

Annette had been to a healer prior to coming to see me. She had then gone to America for laser surgery to treat her endometriosis. When anyone comes to me for a healing, the first thing I try to do is restore the blueprint they were born with and return the chemical messaging system back to its pre-disease condition. When I looked up the condition known as endometriosis in medical books, I could see I was going have to use some Jeannie ingenuity. In endometriosis, adhesions develop and cells start attaching themselves to organs, causing all sorts of problems. Annette's problem at the time involved her kidneys. During her periods, she would be in complete agony. The result of the surgery in America was unsatisfactory. The doctor recommended she be put on the contraceptive pill continuously until she experienced what is known as 'breakthrough bleeding.' Then she would come off the pill for a week of agony.

I told Annette straight out that I really didn't know where to start. For blood clots I normally used the chemical frequency of lemon; for a cyst or tumour, I used the colour indigo. This time, though, I was completely stumped. I balanced all her systems and booked her in for another appointment in a month's time to give me a chance to ponder a plan of action for her disease process.

When I got home, it didn't take me long to get the help I needed to formulate a plan of action. I was told the only thing I could do was repeated birth frequency healings, counselling her in between to remove old emotional patterns and disturbances. Eventually the body would remember its birth song or frequency and the status quo would be achieved. Her cellular renewal and repair system would then work to restore its original blueprint, and the cells creating the condition known as endometriosis would not be reproduced.

Annette had four or five healings with me. She and Iain split up and we became great friends. Her eighty-three-year-old father was booked for an angiogram. As he was on warfarin, a blood thinning agent, they had a problem stemming the blood flow from the incision made for the angiogram. A worried Annette phoned and told me about the problem. I told her what to do with her crystal to help the blood to clot. A couple of days later, she reported that she had immediately sent the healing. The blood had stopped flowing and her father had been allowed to come home that night instead of having to stay in hospital overnight.

Everybody was getting excited about celebrating the Millennium New Year, something for which I just couldn't find enthusiasm. Most of my previous New Years, with the exception of my time with Roger, had been spent in solitude. Iain was determined I wasn't going to spend this one on my own. He was still in the Fire Service and working on the Millennium New Year's Eve. His watch had arranged a party while they were on duty at the Station. He persuaded me to attend, and I persuaded Sally to accompany me. I hate going anywhere on my own, so going to a Fire Station full of fireman was an ordeal that challenged me, to say the least.

Dolled up to the nines and feeling unusually good about myself, I set out for Yarmouth, which was about twenty miles away. Then the voice in my head started, loud, clear, and concise.

"The guy you saw at the gym will be at the Fire Station."

Don't be ridiculous, Jeannie, I told myself. You're getting hyper-nervous and inventing ridiculous fantasies.

I arrived at the Station and phoned Iain on his mobile to come out and meet me. A loud game of snooker was taking place in their lounge room.

"You're early," he said. "There's no one here yet. Come on in and meet the boys."

"Oh!" I said, horrorstruck. "I'll wait in the car until some people arrive. I don't want to be in there on my own with all those strangers."

"Come on, " he said. "You can't sit out here in the cold. I'll take you to a little TV room and you can wait in there."

I settled myself down in front of the TV and made myself as small and inconspicuous as possible. Still the voices persisted. "He's here," they told me. I was having enough of a problem being early and on my own without the added intrusion of these voices telling me the guy from the gym was here.

I flicked the TV channels and tried to look nonchalant. People were walking past the room and poking their heads in to say hi to me. Then it happened. The good-looking guy from the gym walked in and sat down directly opposite me. He politely acknowledged me without really looking at me and began reading a paper. I grabbed the nearest magazine and hid behind it until he had gone. I told Iain what had taken place. He said the guy wasn't on his watch and was a bit of a womanizer.

So that was that. There are no coincidences. That little incident was enough to teach me to always expect the unexpected and to listen to my intuition and trust it, no matter how farfetched it may seem. I am reminded of two incidents that took place in my youth at the ages of fourteen and twenty-one. (I had a theory that life seemed to run in seven-year cycles. Iain White's book on Australian Flower Essences has a chapter at the beginning that deals with this phenomenon.)

My experience at fourteen occurred while driving from Norwich to London after a weekend visit with my mum and dad's brothers and sisters. I kept getting a flash vision in my head, as though our car were on tram tracks. No matter what I did or how I tried to block it, the vision recurred again and again. As we neared London in the dark, the car headlights shone a path for us to follow. Suddenly our car swerved violently and we heard a loud ripping noise in the back. We stopped as soon as we could, and Dad got out to investigate. An oncoming car turning right had crossed too far over the white line and we had almost collided. Fortunately, only the rear bumper had been torn off, but it had been a close call. I wondered if my flash vision had been a warning to stay tight in our own lane. I had always been a strange child, and although I had managed to shut down my sixth sense, it still came to the fore when required. I plucked up the courage to tell Dad about my vision prior to the accident. He said he wished I had told him so he could have taken precautions and moved further over to the left. I told him I had no idea what the vision meant at the time.

At the age of twenty-one, I had a flash vision of a blue car hitting a brick wall. By then, I knew to start panicking at the first sign of any such vision. Dad often drove various cars from the pool of cars at his workplace. After I told him about my vision, he said under no circumstances would he get in a blue car. Of course, I overlooked the fact that I drove a blue car. Two months later, I had the accident. Fortunately, I didn't hit a brick wall and the damage was only to the car.

These two incidents served to make me even more paranoid when my sixth sense tried to help me. I became a complete worrier, imagining the worst scenario in every situation and then wondering if it was one of my flashes foretelling disaster. I began playing all sorts of mind games with myself in an attempt to achieve some kind of peace and balance.

Over the previous twelve years in my development as a healer, I had learned to listen to my sixth sense and dissolve my paranoia and fears. Thanks to Jeremy, the spiritual teacher, and my dad's common sense simplicity philosophy, I was also careful to check out everything I was told and accept only what my gut instinct told me was okay. With the help of the Seraphim, I formulated a system by which I knew I could work safely without "on the side" interference. I also learned how to use my 'flashes' to my advantage.

My friend Sally was encountering a few difficulties in her life. It seemed like a good idea for her to talk to Natalie, my friend in Australia, as Natalie had been through the same development process I had gone through and understood the emotional toll it could take on a person's life. The result of this liaison was an excited phone call from Sally.

"We have to go to Australia, Jeanne," she said.

"Okay," I replied. "Are you absolutely sure?"

"Yes!" Sally replied. "I've never been so sure of anything."

I waited a couple of weeks to give her some time to calm down. I had borrowed some money to fix the dilapidated building that housed my kitchen. I told myself if I was meant to go to Australia, it was okay to use that money. I phoned Sally and asked her if she was sure she wanted me to book the ticket.

"Yes, I'm sure," she replied.

I booked our tickets. I had meant to book hers for two weeks and mine for three weeks, but I ended up booking hers for three weeks and mine for four. The ticket clerk had informed me at the time of booking that the tickets were the only ones left and if I booked them there and then, there would be no refund. I swallowed hard and made the booking. There was no going back.

After I booked the tickets, Sally decided she really didn't want to go to Australia. She also had a problem with my booking her trip for three weeks instead of two. She became somewhat defensive and aggressive about the subject, so I retreated and left her to work it out for herself. We had very little contact up until two days before our departure when I phoned her to make the final arrangements. We were going to stay with Natalie and Adam, whom Sally didn't know very well. My disgruntled friend and I boarded the plane on the day of departure. I sensed her dread at having to spend the next three weeks in Australia with strangers. It was an all-too-familiar feeling.

We were met at the airport by an ecstatic Nat and Adam. Eventually, Sally's mood improved and she started to relax, as the conversation between the four of us flowed and the enthusiasm and excitement Nat and Adam were exhibiting began to infect both of us. We arrived on a Wednesday evening and spent all day Thursday resting. When Teresa phoned me to say hi, I immediately asked her when she could take us to the Adyar again.

"Tomorrow I will take you both on the train," she replied.

I could hardly contain my excitement at my impending visit to the Adyar. When we arrived at the Adyar the next morning, I left my bag with Teresa and off we went.

"Take as long as you like," she told us. "I have all day."

I found a couple of books on angels. As usual, I had glanced at a page in each book before deciding to purchase them. I had filled my basket with an assortment of books when a large cream-coloured one caught my eye.

The front cover had the letters YHWH displayed in gold with a set of wings underneath and hands and lines descending from those wings. This is the reason I came here, I told myself. When I picked up the book, it fell open at a certain page, which I read quickly. I knew the book was for me, but I was shocked when I looked at the price: $112.50. It was called The Book of Knowledge, The Keys of Enoch by J.J. Hurtak.

By the time we arrived home, I was exhausted and didn't give my purchases another thought. Later on, Nat and Adam arrived home from work. We had our meal and went to bed early. The following morning, we would visit Bungan Beach with Nat, Adam and their dogs, three Staffies, Jeannie, Harry, and Chelsea.

The next morning we set out in the car for Bungan Beach, which turned out to be at the bottom of a very steep drop. To get there, we had to walk down many steps. I couldn't help wondering how I would get back up those steps. I was accustomed to stopping for a breather even during mild forms of exercise, let alone climbing the equivalent of four staircases.

After dipping our toes in the sea, I left the three of them to go and sit on the towels we had put down on the sand. As I watched them chatting together, I smiled to myself. At last, all the pieces of the jigsaw were coming together. These three people had watched me develop the tools for CCDH and now, although from opposite sides of the world, here they were, all of them CCDH Masters and conversing together for the first time. That's it, I told myself. I had gotten CCDH off the ground, and they would take it forward. I fell into a deep sleep right there on the beach. I awoke about an hour later just as they were coming to lay with me on the towels.

"How about a meditation?" I asked

All three were enthusiastic, so I began. I had envisaged a normal start to the meditation, but as soon as I began I knew it would be different. I was taken on a completely new visual journey, and became aware of a slight variation in the energy that was guiding me. My gut instinct told me it was alright to proceed. I attributed my strange feelings to the fact I was on the other side of the world.

As the meditation began, the three of them visualized they were flying to a planet called Arcturus.

I had been given strange things to say in meditations before. One time I was told to tell everyone that when they left a room in the building at the top of the mountain, a huge eagle would be waiting to fly them down and they were to hop onto it. As the words arrived in my head, I remained silent for a while to make sure I had understood correctly, struggling with how I would voice it. In the end, I just said it as I had been told. When everybody came out of the meditation, I was amazed at the number of people who said that that they had gone outside before I even mentioned it and the eagle had been there waiting for them. They had hopped on the eagle, which had flown them down the mountain before I said it would. From my past experiences in groups, I had learned to conduct meditations exactly as they were presented to me, no matter how weird they might seem at the time. There was always a good reason for it.

The meditation on Bungan Beach proceeded with my giving the three advanced students a formula by which they could visualize their cellular patterning, begin clearing any obstructions, and make affirmations as to what they wanted to do with their lives. At the end of the meditation, Nat told me her experience had been very different from what she normally experienced during my meditations. In fact, all three of them were so blown away by the experience they fell into a deep sleep within minutes.

I was curious but unruffled by this turn of events. My training to date had included many situations that had been designed to build my trust in myself and my sixth sense, or gut instinct.

On the way home I received another communication. This time it was the name of a place.

"That's Berowra," Natalie said. "It has a huge park where we can walk to a very special place. We'll go there tomorrow."

I climbed up from the beach, taking frequent breathers along the way. After we had something to eat in a little café, we were glad to get home and hit the sack.

The next day was Sunday. We had arranged to rise early and drive to Berowra. When we arrived, Nat told me it was quite a long walk to their special place. I told her I would be fine if we took our time. We walked for some time with Adam leading the way until we came to a huge rock about the size of a small house.

The four of us sat together in a close cluster. I looked out over the huge expanse of water in front of us and saw an Angel so big it rose from the water right up to the sky. I informed the other three of the presence of the Angel. As I did so, it moved towards us. The energy and the close proximity of this giant being of light caused Adam to gasp out loud and move back several feet from the rest of us. Suddenly both girls began to see patterns and symbols in the water, and began to describe what they were seeing. At last, I thought, others are witnessing what I have seen so often. Thank God they could share this beautiful experience with me.

As we walked back to the car, dazed by the experience, I could see beautiful green patches of light floating around us. The energy had affected Adam so dramatically that he had to stand for a moment and steady himself against a tree trunk.

"I think we have a new Angel," I said, as Sally walked up beside me. "I'm not sure if it is one or a group of Angels, but the name is Ophanim."

Sally nodded and nothing more was said.

Unbeknownst to me, I would meet more wonderful Angelic hosts.

The next morning after Adam and Nat had gone to work, I remembered the cream YHWH book that I had purchased but not yet started to read. I opened it and began reading. Sally sat opposite me, engrossed in one of her purchases from the Adyar.

I turned the page and gasped out loud. The Introduction of the book began with the author meeting an Angel called Master Ophanim Enoch. After reading further, I was able to establish that the Ophanim was in fact another group of Angels. In the Introduction, the author was flown to Arcturus, purportedly a reprogramming station. My meditation on Bungan Beach now became clear. How glad I was that I had trusted my guidance and conducted the meditation exactly as it had been given to me. The entire meditation now made sense to me, including the bit where I had asked my students to clean up their cellular patterning and make the affirmations. This was certainly turning out to be a different trip from my first visit to Australia. This piece of information alone was enough to make the whole journey worthwhile.

During the ensuing week, I was again given a location. This resulted in us taking a trip to some mountains in Sydney called The Three Sisters. Every time we set out on one of these weekend trips, our energy and excitement was palpable. We arrived at a car park and set out for a lookout point that would give us a good view of the mountains. A set of steps led down to a railed platform overlooking a huge, deep canyon of trees and Australian bush land.

Sally and Nat stood on either side of me and I put my hands on the middle of their backs, level with their heart centres. I instructed them to close their eyes and go with me. I was told to visualize myself flying with them into the centre of a huge Angel, much like the one at Berowra. I was not to mention a word about what I was doing; I was to tell them to breathe deeply and go with the energy they were feeling from my hands on their backs. I then visualized myself travelling up and over the barrier and into the Angel. To me, this felt like flying in an airplane and then leveled out. I had a vision of Nat and Sally flying around over the great canyon, happy and free as birds in the energy field of this giant Angel. Our eyes remained closed for about ten minutes, as we savoured the experience. When it felt like the time was right, I visually flew them back onto the lookout where the whole experience had begun.

I shook myself out of my trance, opened my eyes, and looked at the girls.

"There's an angel over there!" they exclaimed excitedly, pointing to where I had seen it. "I flew right into it and had a great time flying around in that energy," they said at the same time." They stared at each other, realizing they had both experienced exactly the same thing.

This was real. This was the stuff of fairytales, and it was happening to us.

We made our way to a bench at the foot of the steps and flopped down on it. I saw another smaller angel and got each one of my colleagues to tune in to it as I had taught them. Each one received a communication that was specific to them. There was no word in the English language to describe how I felt at that moment. At last, other human beings were sharing with me firsthand what I had experienced in different ways all my life.

Nat had taken a couple of days off, so we visited different beach locations. I couldn't resist playing with my new healing tool. I would place Nat's hand on mine and take her on a silent visual journey, experimenting with different levels of energy. Without fail, she would break away when she became uncomfortable, and then accurately describe where I had taken her with only my thoughts.

On my first visit to Australia, I had been taken to the Buddhist Temple in Woolangong, where I had received a communication from an unseen being at each of the five statues in the huge temple there. I knew Sally and I needed to visit Woolangong together. On the third weekend of our visit, -- Sally's last weekend in Australia -- we set out for Woolangong. The journey took about an hour and a half. Every time I looked at Sally, she had her eyes closed. My friend Sally, who had not believed she could send lemon to areas nine and ten on the suicidal guy, when I had first begun teaching her, was now closing her eyes and luxuriating in the energies that were engulfing us as we headed for Woolangong. This time I knew what to do before I got there, and I was eager to get on with it.

We walked up the steps to the courtyard and then around to the big temple that housed the five huge statues. As we stood in front of the first statue, oblivious to the large number of visitors walking around the temple, I asked my friends to close their eyes. I told them what the statue in front of them represented and asked them to make their affirmation as to what they wanted in their life in accordance with what that statue represented. I have absolutely no memory of what I said; I just remember Adam swaying so violently I feared he would fall over. I managed to stifle a giggle. Nat and Sally were also swaying back and forth as if in the grips of some incredible force, but not as much as Adam.

As we stood in front of each of the five statues, we recited the meaning of each statue and our individual affirmations based on what we had chosen for our future life paths. Then we left the huge building. As usual, silence fell over the four of us as we pondered the magnitude of what had just happened.

Adam disappeared for awhile. When he returned he grinned at me and said, "You were spot on, Jeannie."

"What are you talking about?" I asked.

"I just went and had a look at the meaning of each statue written on the wall outside," he replied, "and you were bang on."

"Oh, I didn't know that," I replied. "I just shared it as it came, like I always do."

"I know," he said.

That afternoon saw us visiting yet another magical site -- a beach with a very steep descent. Sharp clusters of volcanic rock jutted out from the sea. Our need to reach the furthest possible point on the sharp jagged rocks consumed each one of us as we climbed silently over them. When we arrived, we lay down and fell asleep. (It was only when we were both back in the UK that Sally told me she hadn't been able to see a thing when she was clambering over those rocks. She had had trouble with her vision ever since leaving the temple at Woolangong.)

The time had come for Sally to return to England. I had another week left, which I desperately needed to recover from the events of the past three.

Just before I returned to the UK, Nat, Adam, and I went to a coffee house overlooking the river we had visited earlier with Sally. At that time, we had watched two eagles flying backwards and forwards across the lake, presumably on fishing expeditions. This time the eagles were just off in the distance.

Darkness is only Light not Switched On

"I'll try and communicate with them," I said to Nat and Adam, closing my eyes and willing the eagles to fly over us so we could get a good look at them. Within minutes the awesome, majestic birds were circling over our heads, and continued to do so until we left.

On my return trip home alone, I stopped off in Bangkok and got on another plane to the UK. I had come a long way since taking the train to Liverpool instead of Liverpool Street.

What had I learned?

(1) To share exactly what comes in complete trust.

(2) The Seraphim, and now a new group of Angels, were giving me all I needed to help my students in ways beyond my wildest imagination.

(3) To balance what came via my sixth sense and gut instinct.

(4) I didn't need Dad to be here to be able to travel the world.

What was the Universe teaching me?

I had all the support I needed. All I had to do was trust completely and step forward without fear.

CHAPTER 13

Walking back to Life

After my illness covered in the beginning of the book, when I was well enough, I left the hospital and returned home. Iain and I had redecorated my bedroom. My waterbed, which held many bad memories for me, was put out on the manure heap and burned. I felt massive relief as I watched that old bed go up in flames. I had shared my bed in that room with my ex-husband and Roger, and both were gone from my life now. It was time to wipe the slate clean. Redecorating my bedroom proved to be a cleansing experience.

The loneliness I felt at Roger's departure was again haunting me. The sadness felt like a blanket engulfing me. I wanted to stay and learn to enjoy life, but I didn't know where to start.

The voices in my head began again.

"Go and see David," they told me.

I had met David three years earlier while visiting Warren with Nat and Teresa. We shook hands and a kind of knowing had passed immediately between us. At the time, David told me he had been very ill and was only just recovering. When he mentioned the Masters of Wisdom, I enthusiastically told him about my first visit to Australia and my discovery of the books written about them. I had visited David on several occasions over the years since that first meeting. Eventually, my visits became few and far between, when the voices told me in no uncertain terms to go visit him.

My voices were again insisting that I go to David and seek help. My experience with men in general had not been great, so this was advice I didn't want to heed. In the end, though, while in the depths of despair over which direction to take in my life, I went to pick up horse feed just down the road from where David lived. On a whim, I drove to his house. I parked my car and sat there for a moment, wondering what I would say to him. I decided not to go in and searched for my car keys, which I had removed from the ignition and put down somewhere in the car. I couldn't find the keys anywhere.

"Okay, I said out loud. "I'll go in and see him."

David greeted me with the usual hug and expressed his surprise at how well I looked. He had not visited me in hospital, but Nat and Sally had been in touch with him and had told him how ill I was. That they had managed to get in touch with him at all surprised me, since we were no more than acquaintances. I told him that I felt I lacked the support to take CCDH forward.

"You don't have to," was his immediate response. "Take time out and just *be*."

He asked me when I had first felt this lack of support. I recognized the familiar pattern of Mum never acknowledging or questioning why she deemed me a strange child. Up until then, David had never shown me that he had an inclination to a heal. I learned that he had taken a course in NLP -- Neuro Linguistic Programming -- something I, too, had decided to study. I was extremely embarrassed to suddenly find myself in floods of tears with a man I hardly knew. David definitely saw my vulnerable side that day.

Our chat ended after I got all the painful feelings off my chest. David said he would help in any way he could and invited me to a talk he was doing on a series of courses he had undertaken with his partner.

Always searching for ways to heal myself, I agreed to attend the talk; however, I learned nothing new there, and decided that attending his courses would not help me.

The voices came again. "Ask David to help you," they said.

After some gentle prodding and pushing by the voices, I eventually asked David if he would use his NLP to help heal me, and he agreed. I telephoned him and we booked three or four appointments.

I arrived at the first appointment feeling nervous and vulnerable. Slowly David earned my trust and I began to open up in a way I had never opened up to any male before. I even surprised myself. David helped me to find the seeds of my desire to exit this planet. I still needed to find an exciting reason to stay, but he couldn't help me with that; it was clearly my choice to make. I must admit I was infuriated when people told me to 'take it easy and just *be*' when I explained to them that I was searching for something to do. I was eager to pick up the pieces of my life and begin again. Taking it easy and 'just being' was not my style.

On Apr 5, 2002, I had an appointment to see my consultant at the heart clinic, a wonderful man with a somewhat open mind to miracles. He came out to collect me from the waiting room. As we walked to his consulting room, he looked at me in surprise.

"You're not breathless," he remarked, increasing his pace.

"No," I replied with a grin.

I must admit returning to the hospital that day made me painfully aware of how ill and vulnerable I had been. I looked at all the people still gasping for breath. Each one seemed to be so miserable and totally consumed with pain. The sight of these people frightened the living daylights out of me. I never wanted to return to that place again.

My consultant sat me in a chair and asked me how I was. I told him I had a slight problem with coordination, which I assumed was due to the fact that my heart had stopped twice. He nodded in agreement and listened to my heart.

"You wouldn't know you've had a problem from listening to that," he commented.

A warm glow filled me. Thanks to my friends Sally and David, I was on the road to recovery. I remember David's first comment when I told him about my diagnosis. The nurse had told me that the heart muscle doesn't recover. David thought that was nonsense and said that the heart was a muscle was like any other muscle; it needed to be exercised correctly for it to find its tone again.

I flashed back to my colour course where we were taught to use orange to strengthen muscle. I had immediately picked up my crystal and programmed in multiple sends of orange to the heart muscle. As far as I was concerned, my knowledge and application of colour frequencies was the one overriding factor that had helped my speedy recovery thus far.

The consultant asked if I would mind meeting his colleague. When I obliged, he disappeared around the corner. As I turned to face the stranger in the doorway, he said to her, "Do you recognize this lady?"

She looked at me and said, falteringly, "It's the lady I resuscitated."

"I've been wanting to give you a hug for bringing me back. Thank you!"

As she turned to head back to her consulting room, I saw the tears in her eyes. My eyes had welled up, too.

My consultant wasn't content to leave things as they were. Despite how well I was feeling, he wanted me to have an angiogram to see what, if anything, was going on.

While I had been in hospital, Iain had promised to not only see that my kitchen was finished, but to also take me on holiday. Thanks to my illness, he had gained newfound respect for his mum's time. It had been twenty years since I had had a decent kitchen with oven, hob, and grill that worked properly. The crystals I owned would have probably paid for a new kitchen had I not bought them, but they were the tools of my trade and I wouldn't be without them.

Iain had left the Fire Service, taken a job with the electrical controls company, and started working at the Norfolk and Norwich Hospital. One day he came home and announced he was unhappy with the way his company was treating him and was going to start his own company. A year earlier, he had formed a limited partnership with a friend, who no longer wanted anything to do with it.

"Find a place for us to go on holiday," he said to me. He would start the company when we got back.

His friends scoffed at the idea of Iain and me peaceably sharing a small room for a week. Our arguments were legendary amongst his mates. He had worked around the clock the week preceding our holiday to Halkidiki, and was very disgruntled as he set out for the airport with me.

He had had no sleep in twenty-four hours and told me to keep talking so he'd stay awake while he drove. I searched for topics of conversation. If only he would let me drive. The stress of trying to keep him awake and prevent us from having an accident was far worse than having to take the wheel. But he would have none of it. Eventually, we pulled into a petrol station where he bought a coffee. He positioned himself for a snooze and asked me to wake him twenty minutes later so we could get to the airport on time. It was two o'clock in the morning. I had no idea if I could keep my own eyes open, let alone wake him.

We finally arrived at the airport. Because of my inability to walk long distances quickly, Iain sent me off to walk ahead of him, as it was a long way to our departure gate. I surprised myself by covering the distance quite quickly, while fending off old memories of other painful approaches to these gates.

When the stewardess took my boarding pass and waved me onto the plane, I boarded the plane after waiting only a short time for Iain. I was going with or without him. I was settled at the back of the plane and becoming more than a little concerned that Iain had not yet arrived when a breathless and angry son walked up to me.

"So you're on the plane, you little monkey," he said. "I told them there was no way my mother would get on that plane without me, but here you are."

We had a good laugh, just as we had done when recounting the events that had him driving down the Southern Bypass with me on January 28th to the hospital where I had then died twice and been revived. While other people found our mirth at such events somewhat disconcerting, we could always see the funny side. Was I finally beginning to find some joy in my life?

We spent the week's holiday enjoying each other's company. Not one argument arose. One day we took a boat trip out to sea. The skipper was throwing people overboard at the place designated for a swim. I was terrified. I had a vivid memory of being in hospital after being released from intensive care. I had been hankering for a cold shower to clear my energy field. When I turned on the cold water, I found myself gasping for breath and feeling faint. My heart hadn't been ready to deal with the shock of cold water on my body. Now here I was in Greece with an opportunity to swim in the very cold sea and enjoy the sunshine and the company of my son. The only thing holding me back was the fear of how the cold water would affect my heart.

Instead of plunging into the sea, I persuaded the captain to let me climb down the steps and slowly lower myself into the cold water. When I did, I swam all the way around the boat. I was reminded of the day I began an improvement course and was asked to focus on a joyful experience in my life. At the time, the only joyful experience I could come up with was a hug from my little dog Lolly. Now I had new experiences from which to draw when creating powerful positive programming exercises. It felt like my life had started anew.

I spent the ensuing months slowly rebuilding my life and my health. I had almost forgotten how ill I had been until the hospital called, wanting to know if I could come for an angiogram the following Thursday. My immediate reaction was to say no, but I stopped myself.

"Yes, I can attend. That will be fine," I said.

What if the angiogram showed I had not healed my heart and my current state of feeling better was just an illusion? The sleepless nights returned, along with the memories of lying in bed unable to breath. The helplessness and loneliness descended upon me once again.

"I'm going to need all the help and support you can muster." I told my angels.

Iain took a couple of days off work to support me. My friend Donna took me to the hospital and Iain had arranged to pick me up. I had been getting a message in my head for days now. The word Carnitine kept repeating over and over again. I had no idea what it was.

On the day of the angiogram, I sat nervously waiting for my turn, pleading for my 'guys' to stay close. As I absentmindedly thumbed through a magazine, I spotted an article about Carnitine. I read that this substance is found in red meat and that a deficiency in it may cause heart problems. When I mentioned this to David, he said I was probably talking about L Carnitine. He had heard of it, but didn't know what purpose it served. This sent him off to research L Carnitine while I searched the Internet. I discovered that the body manufactured Carnitine from certain foods we eat, and if wasn't able to produce enough Carnitine, cardiomyopathy could result. From that day forward, I began eating meat again. (As much as I dislike it, I will eat it to stay healthy. I also discovered that I could eat baby leaf spinach as a salad, so I make sure I ingest plenty of it in an effort to ensure my body is able to manufacture Carnitine.)

I was a bit worried that eating meat would interfere with my communication with the angels. While I still get the help and guidance I need just as clearly, I usually abstain from eating meat before working. I find that eating meat just before a healing or reading changes the frequency at which my physical body is operating, and the 'antennae' that either receives the messages or transmits the healing frequencies (my physical body) is not as accurate or receptive as it is when I have no meat in my system.

The time for my angiogram had come. I was wheeled down on my bed to the waiting room. My own consultant was going to conduct the angiogram. My fight to get up and escape when I'm at death's door is legendary. (It had apparently taken four nurses to hold me down for the doctor to carry out an examination when Iain had finally got me to the hospital on January 28th). I needed to suppress this instinct in order to lie still for the angiogram. I was told to lie as still as I could while they inserted the tube just over my right hip.

"Come on, guys," I called. "I need you now, more than ever. Come on. Come close."

It has been my teaching and experience that angels will only approach us if we and our immediate surroundings are relatively clear of negative ergy. Having positive energy, they draw negative energy to them like fluff to an ionizer. Because they don't have physical bodies, they are unable to process or rid themselves of it. This is why my meetings up close with angels usually took place near water, the Australian Bush, at sea, or somewhere on the eighty acres of Warren's estate.

Each time I felt the urge to rip out the angiogram probe, I called to my guys. In truth, I didn't really think they would come close to me while I was in such a negative environment. But that day they answered my call stronger than ever. I watched the lights dance around the room, penetrate both doctors who were attending me, and then settle in the centre of my chest. A sudden wave of calm fell over the whole room.

"Do you want me to change the music?" asked my consultant.

"Yes," I replied.

Magically, a spiritual melody began to play.

The probe moved across my chest cavity and into the left side of my heart. My wonderful consultant's surprise was easily discernable, even though not much was said out loud. After the procedure, the assisting doctor pressed his hands down hard on the entry wound to stem the bleeding. As the young doctor stood over me, noticeably unsteady and unable to stifle huge yawns, I could see lights dancing around his head and going in and out of his body. We chatted briefly. He mentioned that the consultant had been surprised at the result. I told him I was a healer and had used colour therapy to strengthen the heart muscle. When he asked how I had done it, I explained that I had used a crystal and then programmed the colour in. He started to question me further. I knew if I told him how simple it was, he probably wouldn't believe me.

That evening I waited nervously for the results of the angiogram. My consultant arrived and told me they had found only a furring of the arteries, which didn't explain my condition last January. He sent me to Papworth for a second opinion, as he didn't know what to make of the results and was worried another flu virus might send me back to the hospital. He said the consultant at Papworth might suggest a bypass in order to avoid such an incident.

Some months later, I received a letter from Papworth, informing me that I was on the waiting list for a bypass. I was devastated. I would never turn down such an operation if they thought I needed it, but I had made an affirmation that I would clear my arteries myself if they were clogged from cholesterol. This letter had effectively eradicated my opportunity to find a way to clear the arteries without surgery.

My first phone call was to David, who reassured me that he would do all he could to help. Several days later, I received a letter requesting that I attend an appointment with the consultant at Papworth to discuss the possibility of surgery. Phew, that's better, I thought. At least they're not treating it as 'done deal.' I plucked up the courage to ask David to go with me to Papworth; as he was the only one I trusted to speak up for me. He knew the right questions to ask, and would help me overcome my usual discomfort and awkwardness in these types of situations. He wouldn't be afraid to ask questions or, if need be, challenge what the doctor said. It was a great relief when he agreed to accompany me.

My insomnia returned with a vengeance.

On January 8th, 2003, David and I took the train to Papworth. David's way of looking after me was reminiscent of the way my Dad had always taken care of me but without the emotional control. He reassured me, as I waited nervously to see the consultant. When it was time for my appointment, we entered the consulting room together.

The consultant asked me about the events of my illness and listened as no other doctor had ever done. "Do you have any angina?" he asked.

"No," I replied.

"Then I can see no reason for surgery," he said.

I told him that because my mother had died of a cholesterol-choked heart, I had tried various diets and medication, all to no avail. He said I could eat whatever I wanted (with the possible exception of Norfolk dumplings and suet pudding!) and use medication to reduce my cholesterol level.

David and I hugged each other and danced for joy as we left the consulting room. David had persuaded the taxi driver to wait for us, and there he was, ready and waiting to take us back to the train station.

This news of my clogged arteries brought to the fore all the information I had gathered after Mum had died. I looked to my system of healing for an answer. I could find only part of the answer. I was given a colour to programme in, but I knew it would not be enough to deal with my problem. I researched how cholesterol is produced in the body. My conclusion was that birth frequency healing would not help me in this instance. Some cases of high blood cholesterol were hereditary. I have since found out that you need to ingest fat to be able to process fat; otherwise, the body just stores it for use later (which explains 'love handles'!). If I was born with the genetic predisposition to high cholesterol, then returning to my birth frequency programming would certainly not help me. In all probability, I've had a high cholesterol count since birth.

I resolved to make a nighttime affirmation to find a way to deal with my problem. Again, I found myself at David's door searching for a way to clear the problem. After looking at my mum and her emotional life, I concluded that cholesterol represented 'emotional gunk' in a person's life. I had done so much to delete this gunk; I wondered what more I could possibly do.

David suggested I see one of his friends who was a homeopath. I made an appointment with the homeopath, who told me to write a short life history before my visit. I arrived for the session, armed with a short appraisal of my life to date. He asked me what I had done in Australia. When I told him about the Angels, I expected him to be shocked. I was pleasantly surprised when he didn't bat an eyelash. Encouraged by his openness, I held nothing back as he questioned me.

At one point, when he questioned me about a particular aspect of the sense of responsibility I felt, I was unable to express my feelings. When the Angels intervened to help me understand and convey my innate feelings of loneliness and separation, the homeopath almost burst into tears. In that moment, I understood the huge burden of responsibility I had felt for my parents' happiness, even before I was born. I could see why I had always been so sad. In that instant, the homeopath felt and saw it, too.

The homeopath sent me away, promising a remedy would arrive in the post. When I asked him how the remedy would help address my cholesterol levels, he replied, "Get rid of the gunk in your life and you'll get rid of the cholesterol." That did it for me. I had found a homeopath -- a fellow Aquarian (his birthday was the day before mine) whose philosophy regarding the healing process appeared to be similar to mine.

The homeopathic remedies healed in their own special way. Their frequencies were definitely what I needed to assist me in removing the gunk from my cellular patterning and emotional responses so I could really enjoy being alive. In order to teach the world to sing, I had to feel like singing myself.

What had I learned?

(1) That I am still and always will be learning.

What was the universe teaching me?

To sing and experience and remember joy.

Darkness is only Light not Switched On

Contact the Author through CCDH website ccdh.co.uk

Cover photograph by Stephen Herd, Herdy Photography Pty Ltd
Email: stephen.herd@optus.net.au

Acknowledgements

Thanks to my friend Steve for the cover picture - one of many treasures he has captured - with help to be in the right place at the right time from his Angel friends.:

Thanks to my friend Lolita for her constant help and encouragement in project ccdh and for allowing me to use her as my guinea pig on many occasions.

Thanks to my son Iain for his loyal support and help throughout this project.

Thanks to all the animals who have come into my life to share it and give me the unconditional love my soul needs to find the joy and strength it requires to stay.

Thanks to all my students without whose presence and participation to the journey would have been impossible

The Author wishes to make it clear that at no time should anyone who is experiencing health problems go to the Angels for help without seeking the help and advice of a qualified medical practitioner. All Angel help and technology described in this book is supportive of orthodox medicine without which the Author would not be here to tell the story!

ISBN 1-41205508-3